Growing in Grace: The Journey of Discipleship

ASHLEY MERCK

Growing in Grace: The Journey of Discipleship

Copyright © 2023 by Ashley Merck

Cover Design Copyright © 2023 by Ashley Merck

All rights reserved.

ISBN: 9798861238434

Imprint: Independently Published

All Scripture quotations, unless otherwise indicated, are taken from the New King James Version. Copyright © 1982 by Thomas Nelson, Inc. Used by permission. All rights reserved.

Scripture quotations marked NIV are taken from the HOLY BIBLE, NEW INTERNATIONAL VERSION®. Copyright © 1973, 1978, 1984 by International Bible Society. Used by permission of Zondervan Publishing House. All rights reserved.

DEDICATION

To my Lord and Savior, Jesus Chirst. May You get all the glory.

CONTENTS

Preface.. i
Introduction... 1

Part 1: Justification.. 8
Chapter 1: Rooted in Salvation................................ 9

Part 2: Sanctification.. 24
Chapter 2: Growing Through the Word..................... 26
Chapter 3: Growing Through Community.................. 45
Chapter 4: Growing Through Serving....................... 60
Chapter 5: Growing Through Missions..................... 73

Part 3: Glorification... 90
Chapter 6: Coming to Fruition in the Coming Kingdom.... 92

A Note From the Author... 100
Acknowledgements... 101
About the Author.. 103
References.. 104
Notes... 106

Preface

To all who read this book,

Thank you for joining me on this journey of discipleship. This may not be a lengthy book, but it is my goal to make sure it is driven by Scripture. I've learned through both my undergraduate and graduate degrees that the Bible is the most important book that anyone could ever read and books like this one are merely tools to help us learn and understand God's precious Word. Throughout this book, I will use Scripture as the basis and build upon it through personal application for us to implement so that we can become better disciples of our Lord Jesus Christ. I pray this book helps you grow in both grace and knowledge of Christ as you seek to become more like Him daily.

Allow me to briefly introduce myself. My name is Ashley and I am a graduate of Southeastern Baptist Theological Seminary (2021) where I earned a Master of Arts degree in Christian Studies. I obtained my Bachelor's degree from North Greenville University (2019) where I majored in Digital Media. Many people don't know what digital media entails, but it essentially covers everything from journalism to graphic design to social media management. During my time at North Greenville, I gained a lot of experience in writing from core classes like English to my major specific classes like News Writing and Editing. While I love writing and feel it's something God has gifted me with, all the papers and news articles I had to write in undergrad weren't always my favorite. In fact, it wasn't until my time at Southeastern and through my coursework there when I rediscovered my passion for writing. I think it's because I was writing on something I was passionate about that made me realize the gift God has given me.

Writing about my faith is a topic I'm so passionate about and could go on and on talking about even in everyday conversations. It was around the beginning of 2021 when I sensed God leading me to potentially write a book. Though I didn't know what that would look like or what it would be about, I knew I just had to do it or at least try my best at making it happen.

I have written this book because it is something I wish I had as a new believer who didn't know a lot about Christian living and discipleship. My goal is to write something simple enough for a new believer to understand, but also practical enough for a mature believer to enjoy as well as they desire to grow in their faith. As I said before, this may not be a lengthy book, but I pray that it will be soaked in Scripture and challenge whoever is reading this to want to become a better disciple of our Lord Jesus. From the time we become a believer we are constantly growing in our walk with the Lord if we allow Him to do so. I cannot wait to begin this journey with you. All glory be to God. I could not even dream of doing this without Him.

Your Friend in Christ,
Ashley Merck

Introduction

The Student Bible Dictionary defines a disciple as a "learner, student, follower, apprentice."[1] Therefore, biblically speaking, a disciple is someone who is a student or follower of Jesus Christ. From the moment we confess our sin and place our faith in Jesus Christ, we become one of His disciples and our desire to know Him more begins to grow immensely. This is where discipleship comes into play. Discipleship is simply striving to become more like Christ in our daily lives by communing with God Himself, building godly habits such as Bible reading, attending and engaging in the local church, and ultimately sharing the good news of Christ with the world. We must realize that discipleship is not something that can be achieved in a day; rather, it is to be cultivated and pursued throughout the life of a believer. Discipleship is an important aspect in the lives of Christians because it is what refocuses us back to our main purpose in life: to glorify God.

Discipleship is very near and dear to my heart. I have seen its amazing implications and have first hand testimonies of just how wonderful discipleship can be. My admiration for this topic began when I was in college. I think my love for it grew during that time in my life, because I had opportunities to watch it play out in both my own life as well as in the lives of others. My junior year of college was the year that I saw what discipleship looked like first hand, because it was that year when God graciously allowed me to become a chaplain at the university

I was attending. To give a little background, a chaplain at North Greenville is someone who is a spiritual leader on campus. Most chaplains serve in their dorms, but there are a few who minister to commuter students. Chaplains would build relationships with the people and share Christ's love with them. My role was serving commuters as I myself was a commuter.

At first, it was challenging, because I didn't have a dorm hall like the rest of the girls, which meant I had to be more intentional in my relationship building. Each week, North Greenville would host a commuter lunch on Thursdays where I would meet fellow commuter girls and try to build a relationship with them. That year, I built so many great friendships and not only did I gain amazing friends, but I also learned what discipleship truly looked like. I would try my best to pour into these girls the truths of the gospel by holding Bible studies and fellowship times where we could gather and pray for each other. It was such a sweet time and a memory I will always cherish. Not only was I pouring into these girls, but I was being poured into through our small group consisting of other chaplains. I think this is key in successful discipleship. If we are pouring out and not being poured into, then we are bound to burn out and grow weary, for we can only pour out so much before we begin to feel empty.

I've come to learn that discipleship should occur in two ways. First, discipleship is individual in the sense that I must cultivate a relationship with God for myself, and to do that, I need to be intentional in learning more about Him through Bible reading and talking to Him through prayer. Secondly, discipleship is communal in the sense that we need each other as the Body of Christ to encourage, pray, and fellowship with one another in order to grow in our relationship with God through corporate worship and small groups.

I have had many other experiences with discipleship over the years, but the chaplain ministry is one that stands out to me and was very transformative for me in my spiritual journey. Since then, I have grown to love the subject of discipleship and it is one I want to discover deeper. I began dreaming of writing a book in January of 2021. As I was brainstorming ideas on what I could write on, this topic kept coming back to me. I knew it was what God was leading me to and I pray He will use this book to glorify Him and Him alone.

As I prayed what the title of the book would be, God placed on my heart 2 Peter 3:18 which reads, "but grow in the grace and knowledge of our Lord and Savior Jesus Christ. To Him be the glory both now and forever. Amen." This verse also happens to be one of my favorite verses and has been one I've referred back to for several years now. 2 Peter 3:18 captures what true discipleship should look like: growing in both grace and knowledge of Christ. But what exactly does that mean? If we look at this verse in its context, we see that Peter is challenging his intended audience to be diligent in their relationship with God, while also warning them of the dangers of falling prey to the false prophets' teachings of that day.

Clearly, following Christ, obeying Him, and growing through grace and knowledge is far better than believing anything the false prophets have to offer or say. The same is true today. This world is filled with false teachers and other distractions that can lead us away from pursuing a deep, meaningful relationship with our Lord Jesus Christ. As genuine believers, we need to be watchful of these harmful distractions, making sure we are staying rooted in the Word and growing in our walk with God daily.

During my drafting process, as I began thinking of how I wanted to tie everything together, I felt God laying on my heart to write this book in a concise and orderly format that would help readers understand the process of discipleship. I want to take a brief moment to explain how this book will be laid out. The process of our salvation and faith journey is made up of three aspects: justification, sanctification, and glorification. My goal with this book is to explain each of these aspects by using the analogy of a tree or a plant. I thought it would be fitting since I titled the book *Growing in Grace*. While I admire the beauty of flowers and trees, I am not a gardener by any means, but I do see a lot of similarities between plants and discipleship. Let me explain.

Discipleship is a journey. It takes time. Though it begins the moment we are saved, discipleship is not something we complete overnight; rather, it's a process that spans the lifetime of a believer and isn't fully accomplished until Christ returns and makes all things new again. The goal of discipleship is to grow in Christlikeness each day with the help of the Holy Spirit living inside us. Like a tree or a plant, discipleship needs to have a firm root in place to grow and once it begins growing, that plant needs essential elements to keep it strong and healthy until it reaches full fruition. Before going any further, let me briefly explain the terminology and the analogy I will be using throughout this book.

As I mentioned before, salvation is made up of three aspects. Many understand these terms as the following: (1) justification – we have been saved, (2) sanctification – we are being saved, and (3) glorification – we will be saved. While a majority of our discipleship journey occurs in the sanctification phase, each section is important as it relates to our journey of becoming more like Jesus. Please refer to the chart below for a better understanding of the terminology and tense that is being used for each aspect.[2]

Aspect	Justification	Sanctification	Glorification
Tense	Past	Present	Future
Action Taking Place	I have been saved from the penalty of sin.	I am being saved from the power of sin.	I will be saved from the presence of sin.

Now let's begin with justification, the first section of this book. Justification is the very beginning of the discipleship journey and happens at the moment of our conversion. It's at that moment when God convicted us of our sin and we repented, placing our faith in Christ. This is where we are rooted and is the core of our foundation. Without justification, we have no basis for discipleship.

The next section will focus on sanctification and will take up a majority of the book's content. Sanctification is the journey between our beginning point as a believer through salvation to the very end, whether it be through Christ calling us home or through His second-coming. This aspect is happening at this very moment. The sanctification portion of our journey is crucial, because this is the part where we are growing and learning to be more like Christ through our daily disciplines and actions. Once we are rooted, we are expected to grow and be well-nourished as we desire to be a better disciple. In this section of the book, we'll look at practical and applicable ways we can grow deeper in our walk with the Lord and in our love for one another.

Lastly, our focus will shift from growth to what it looks like when we reach the end of our discipleship journey. While it may be morbid to think about the end of our lives here on this earth, we see it's actually not morbid at all. We reach the end by experiencing glorification, knowing God in His goodness and mercy will restore creation back to the way it is supposed to be, and we will be made new again. Through glorification, we will be saved, glorifying the Father, Son, and Holy Spirit for all eternity. This is the point in our journey where we reach fruition, become completely mature as believers, and fulfill the destiny God intended from the beginning of time through the work of His Spirit in us.

As you work your way through this book, reflect on your own journey in your walk with the Lord. To aid in your pursuit of growing in grace, there will be reflection questions at the end of each chapter. These questions can be used either to facilitate discussion in a small group setting or as journal prompts for individuals looking to grow deeper in their faith. Think about when you received salvation and how it felt, think about your Bible reading habits and church engagement, think about what you are excited about when Christ returns to make everything new, etc. The journey of discipleship is a unique and glorious one. This journey is filled with great joy, even in the midst of great trials we may face, because we know that each day with the help of the Holy Spirit, we are growing in Christlikeness.

May we all see God's good work in us and have a fresh new desire to grow in both the grace and knowledge of our Lord Jesus that we may become more like Him each and every day.

Part One
Justification

We Have Been Saved

In this first section of the book, we are going to examine aspect one of our discipleship journey, which is justification. Justification simply means God pouring out His mercy and love on humanity, removing their sin debt, and restoring them back into a right relationship with Him through the sacrifice of His Son, Jesus Christ.

Justification is a one-time event which happens the moment of our initial conversion. This phase in our journey is crucial because it is how we become disciples and is ultimately the foundation of our faith. As mentioned in the introduction, I am considering this portion of our journey as the root as it relates to our tree/plant analogy because it is the beginning, our foundation. Without this crucial aspect, we cannot grow and mature as believers.

As you read this chapter, think back to the moment when you trusted in the Lord Jesus and rejoiced in knowing that you are now called a child of God. If you are not a believer, I pray that you will read this following chapter with an open heart and an open mind. God is always up to something good. We just have to be ready to listen and obey His voice.

1
ROOTED IN SALVATION

Every journey has a beginning. The journey of discipleship begins with our salvation. Salvation can be theologically defined as the saving of our souls from sin through the atoning work that Jesus Christ accomplished by dying on the cross and resurrecting from the dead over 2,000 years ago. Through His sacrificial death and resurrection, we can obtain salvation if we confess with our mouths that Jesus is Lord and believe in our hearts that God raised Him from the dead (Romans 10:9). From that moment on, we are adopted into the family of God and our journey of discipleship truly begins.

Salvation is essential in the life of everyone who is a Christian because without it, we cannot even call ourselves Christians. It is the foundation of our faith, the root of why we believe what we believe. I love how Matt Chandler explains justification in his book *The Explicit Gospel*, "Believing the news that God is holy, that you are a sinner, and that Christ has reconciled you to God by his life, death, and resurrection is what justifies you. This is our foundation, our root."[3] Without salvation, our faith and beliefs would have no meaning and no impact. But before we go any further with why salvation is so significant, let's take a step back and look at the gospel message to see why we even need to be saved in the first place.

Before we can obtain salvation, we must first realize the state our souls are in and repent from the sins that are keeping us from the relationship with God as He originally intended in the beginning. Let's examine the point in human history where everything essentially fell apart due to one couple's disobedience. This may be a story you've heard numerous times or it may be your first time hearing it; regardless, it is a point in history where the world changed forever and is worth repeating, so that we can know why we are broken people who live in a fallen world.

Why We Are in Need of Salvation

The story begins with one man, Adam, and one woman, Eve, who were made in the image of God (Genesis 1:26) and lived in the Garden of Eden (Genesis 2:8). In this garden they lived in a perfect relationship with God and with one another, free from sin and death, perfect in every aspect. The LORD instructed them that they could eat of any tree in the garden, except from the tree of the knowledge of good and evil, for if they ate from it they were sure to die (Genesis 2:17). One day in the garden Satan, disguised as a serpent, came and asked Eve, "Has God indeed said, 'You shall not eat of every tree of the garden'?" to which Eve responds with the words the LORD instructed them (Genesis 3:1-3). The serpent, however, continued to persuade her to do otherwise stating that God wanted them to eat from it for their eyes would be opened and they would be like God (Genesis 3:4-5). And with that persuasion Eve took a bite from the fruit of the forbidden tree and offered fruit to Adam as well, to which he also took a bite (Genesis 3:6).

In an instant their lives were changed forever and not just their lives, but the lives of all who would come after them. In that moment they felt instant shame and tried to hide from God, but it did no good. God knew where they were and because of Adam and Eve's disobedience, the LORD gave a punishment that not only affected them but all of humanity. Adam's punishment was that he would have hard, physical labor as he worked and Eve's punishment would be that she would experience pain in childbearing (Gen. 3:16-19). Even the serpent received punishment for his wrongdoing and God cursed him by making him crawl on his belly forever (Gen. 3:14-15).

Adam and Eve may not have experienced an instantaneous death that day, but with their sin they experienced a spiritual death, a separation from God that they had not experienced before. One day they would experience physical death, but for now they were separated from the Father and had no way to reconcile back to the relationship they once had. Because of this, we now all experience both physical death and spiritual separation from God due to our innate sin nature.

The Good News

If the story ended right here, it would be a very sad ending. Thankfully, this isn't the end of our redemption story, as there is a glimmer of hope found within the same chapter of Genesis. In verse 15 of Genesis 3, we see God's first promise of the coming Messiah. This verse is often referred to as the *protoevangelium,* or first gospel, as it is the first reference to Jesus we see in Scripture. In this passage, God is giving the serpent's punishment for his wrongdoings. One of the punishments is God putting enmity between Satan and the woman, between his offspring and hers. But here's where it gets interesting, we know now through Scripture that Jesus is the offspring referenced in this passage, and though Satan will bruise His heel, Jesus will crush Satan's head as promised in this verse. God's salvation plan was established from the very beginning and He made that perfectly clear through this one verse. Though the trajectory of human history has completely shifted from what God had originally intended because of human sin, He still made a way for us to come back into a right relationship with Him through the sacrifice of His only Son, Jesus Christ. He is our only way to obtain salvation.

Through God's amazing grace, all are able to come to faith and obtain salvation. We see throughout the Old Testament that those who placed their faith and trust in God looked forward to the day of Christ's first coming. The LORD foreshadowed His Son's coming through various customs (such as animal sacrifice), feasts (such as Passover), and godly figures (such as David) that would remind His people of what was to come. Though God's redemption plan through the cross had not come into fulfillment, those who placed their faith and trust in the LORD obtained salvation in the Old Testament. Flashforward to the New Testament when Christ appeared on the scene, lived a sinless life, and laid down His life so that we may be reconciled back in the right relationship with God. The plan God promised in the very beginning after the fall of man was now accomplished through the work of Christ.

How amazing is that? We no longer have to live in the shame and guilt of our sin, but can live in freedom and unity with the Father, Son, and Holy Spirit. It's all because of the Lord's precious gift of grace. The Apostle Paul reminds us in Ephesians 2:8, "For it is by grace you have been saved, through faith – and this is not from yourselves, it is the gift of God" (NIV).

A Gift from God

Salvation is a gift from God, a gift that should not be taken for granted. We, who were once so indulged in our sin and hellbound, are saved by grace through the precious blood of the Savior, Who covers every single sin, past, present, and future. We, who are redeemed, are now heavenbound with a bright future ahead of us. Does this mean we will never sin again? Absolutely not. In fact, it's impossible for us to not sin as we are natural born sinners. However, our identity now is that we are sinners who are redeemed and reconciled because of grace.

So what must one do to obtain this free gift from the Lord? Do we have to do certain tasks or have certain abilities or attributes to obtain salvation? No, absolutely not. In fact, it's the exact opposite. The beauty of Christianity is that it is not a works based religion like all other religions. Other religions say to do this or do that in order to make it to heaven or whatever they believe about the afterlife, but not Christianity. Christianity reveals that there is only One Man who is the Way, the Truth, and the Life, and there is no way to the Father except through Him and His name is Jesus (John 14:6). It is through His redemptive work on the cross and resurrection that we can truly obtain salvation.

There is absolutely nothing we can or cannot do to earn salvation. That is why it is called a gift. We sinners who deserve God's wrath instead receive salvation because of His good grace and mercy. Now that's powerful!

In order to receive salvation, we must be aware of the sin in our lives and understand the gospel of Christ. As mentioned before, we are all born with a sin nature, nobody is perfect (except Christ). We must recognize our sin debt and repent before the Father. This, however, is not possible without the work of the Third Person of the Trinity, the Holy Spirit.

The Holy Spirit plays a key role in our conversion experience. Once we have heard the gospel message of Christ's redemptive work, the Holy Spirit begins to work in our lives through conviction of our sin. We may have heard the gospel once or multiple times, but one thing is certain, the Holy Spirit will begin His work when He is ready. Salvation doesn't happen on our timetable; it happens on God's timetable. If it happened when we wanted it to happen, then we would never be ready and would always be making an excuse, but not God. Once He convicts us of our sins, we have a very important decision to make. We can either be receptive to what the Lord is placing on our hearts, repent of our sins, and trust in Him or we can ignore it, move on, and forget it even happened. Upon our decision to receive salvation, the Holy Spirit then takes up residence in our hearts, empowering us in our pursuit of a godly life.

The Parable of the Sower

Jesus reminded His listeners of the ways in which people respond to God's Word through a parable in Matthew 13:1-23. A parable is simply a short story to convey a spiritual message, kind of like how pastors use illustrations in their sermons to make a point. In this passage, Jesus tells the multitude a parable about a sower. In the story, the sower throws seeds and they land in different places, which have different consequences. For instance, some fell by the wayside where birds came and ate them. Some fell on stony places where there wasn't much soil and were scorched by the sun, because there was no root for them. Some fell in thorns where the thorns choked them. But there were some that fell on good soil and they flourished because of it.

As Jesus told this story, some did not understand what He meant and questioned why He spoke in parables. He then explains that parables help make the mysteries of the Kingdom more understandable and in verses 18-23, He goes on to explain the significance of the sower parable. The seed represents the Word of God and the different soils represent those who have heard God's Word and how they receive it.

According to Jesus, the wayside is whoever hears the Word of God and does not understand it, the wicked one snatches away what was sown in the heart. The stony places are those who receive the Word joyfully, but have no root to endure long term when trials come their way. Those among the thorns hear the Word, but care more about what the world has to offer and; therefore, they do not produce fruit. Lastly, those who receive the Word on good soil are those who hear it, understand it, bear fruit, and endure until the end.

Through this parable, we realize that we are all one of these soils. Whether we are the wayside, the stony place, the thorns, or the good soil, we resonate with one of these. However, it is ultimately up to us what we decide to do once the seed (the Word of God) is received in our lives. We can either ignore it or receive it with great joy and be rooted in a firm foundation. What is your decision?

How to Obtain Salvation

Throughout this chapter so far, we've examined what salvation means, why we need it, and how it is a gift from God. But how do we obtain salvation exactly? Is it by walking down the aisle at the end of a sermon? Is it through what some call "The Sinner's Prayer"? Honestly, you will not find these methods in the Bible. Even though these methods are helpful when leading someone to Christ, there is no set prayer that we must pray or benediction that we must respond to in order to receive salvation. Scripture simply states that we receive salvation through our sincere faith by *confessing* with our mouths that Jesus is Lord and *believing* in our hearts that God raised Him from the dead (Romans 10:9, *emphasis mine*) as well as *repenting* from our sins (Acts 2:38, *emphasis mine*).

To obtain salvation, the Bible simply says that we must confess, believe, and repent. Those who have attended Vacation Bible School probably know this truth by the salvation ABCs, making it easier to remember the steps.

- A stands for admitting to God that you're a sinner in need of a Savior.

- B stands for believing in Jesus as your Savior, that He died and rose again for your sins.
- C stands for confessing with your mouth that Jesus is Lord.

Praise God that He made a way for us to be set free from the bondage of sin through the sacrifice of His own Son, Jesus Christ. Christ did all the work by dying on a cross and defeating sin and death by resurrecting. All we have to do is genuinely believe in our hearts that He indeed is our Savior. The beautiful thing about salvation is that once we obtain it, it can never be taken away from us. That, my friends, is why it is the most wonderful gift anyone can ever receive, freed from our sin debt and reconciled back to God, who loves us so very much. If you have not received God's free gift of salvation, I pray you do that today.

Forever a Child of God

Once you trust in King Jesus by faith, you are now called a child of God. There is absolutely nothing you could ever do or not do that can take away His love for you. I love how Paul describes God's love in Ephesians 1:5-6: "having predestined us to adoption as sons by Jesus Christ to Himself, according to the good pleasure of His will, to the praise of the glory of His grace, by which He made us accepted in the Beloved." Did you catch the word adoption? When God saves us, we are then adopted into His family.

Think of its significance for just a moment. Here in America and around the world, there are many children who are living in foster care, waiting for someone to adopt them. They are living with no stability as they are continually being moved from home to home from one foster parent to another, no permanent residence, no place to truly call home. They long for someone to love them, care for them, and protect them. Then Lord willing, they receive the answer to their prayers, and a family decides to adopt them as their own. They finally have a place to permanently call home and people who they can call their family. And the beautiful thing is that their age, the color of their skin, or their gender should not matter as they are welcomed in their new families. All that matters is love.

It's the same with us. Prior to becoming a believer, we are like foster children longing for love, care, and protection. We may not immediately run to God as we should, and instead, seek out what we are longing for through other people or materialistic things, but these things ultimately fail us. Then, one day when the Holy Spirit finally grabs a hold of our hearts and we become receptive to His leading, we trust in Christ and then we are adopted into the family of God. Now when God sees us, He does not see a misled child on the path to destruction; rather by His grace, He sees Christ in us and from then on we are called sons and daughters of the King. We are unconditionally loved, cared for, and protected for all eternity through Christ's shed blood for us on the cross. And our age nor skin tone nor gender matter at all as He welcomes us in. All that matters is His love and that is more than enough.

Everyone Has a Story to Tell

I've always been drawn to storytelling. Anyone who knows me knows I'm a big fan of Disney and I think part of it is because they are incredible storytellers. There's just something about seeing a story come to life in front of you and resonating with the characters as you see them in both triumphs and trials. But you know what I find amazing? Every single soul on this Earth has a unique story to be told. Whether they are believers or not, people have stories that need to be told and heard.

As a Christian, I believe that my story of how God saved me from my sin and called me as His own is a very important one that I need to share with those who may not believe the same things I do. This story is often called our testimony as we are testifying to others the work God has done in our lives. Once we become a believer, we have a testimony that needs to be shared. Our testimonies can be a powerful tool when talking to someone who doesn't have a relationship with Jesus or can be an encouragement to fellow believers in the faith.

While everyone's testimony will be a bit different, the central message will be the same: I once was a sinner separated from God, but now I'm saved by His grace and living for His glory. As you prepare to tell your testimony, let's look at the different parts that make up a testimony. A testimony is a story of your life told in usually three distinct sections: (1) your life before coming to saving faith in Christ, (2) how you came to saving faith in Christ, and (3) your life after coming to saving faith in Christ. Let's briefly look at these three components in more detail.

The first section of one's testimony is that person's life before coming to saving faith in Christ. Essentially, this is what your life looked like as a non-believer. Now you may be thinking "but I've grown up in church my whole life and have heard the gospel numerous times, how can I testify about my life before Christ?" Everyone has had a time in their life before they came to know Christ in a personal way whether they grew up in church or not. Simply think about how your life was before coming to know Christ. Were you more anxious? Were you more timid? Were you a people pleaser? Were you without hope? The list could go on and on, but the main point here is to think of what your life was like without Christ in it.

Next in your testimony is recounting how you came to saving faith in Christ, your salvation story. Right before you came to know Jesus, how did you know your need for salvation? How did you hear the gospel message? Also share details of your conversion story if you remember them.

The last part of your testimony is your life after receiving salvation. Just like the section of your life before Christ, here you share what your life has been like since knowing Christ. What changes have you seen in your life since you received salvation? Think back to your life before Christ. If you were anxious, maybe now you feel at peace. If you felt hopeless, maybe now you feel hopeful. Explain how Christ is the reason you feel and know these things to be true. Though it's amazing to hear how Christ transformed your life, also share how just because you are now saved doesn't mean you don't experience pain, heartbreak, and suffering anymore. Jesus never promised us an easy life, He only promised that He will be with us when life doesn't go as planned.

As we have discussed the importance of our testimony, I would like to share a little bit of mine. I didn't grow up in church, but my parents are Christians and I knew about Jesus as I used to read stories in the children's Bible I had. When I was thirteen, I remember sitting on my bed listening to my iPod and I came across this Christian song, and the lyrics really made me ponder about faith. The song was "I Can Only Imagine" by MercyMe and as I listened to the chorus, I began wondering where I would go if I died. Would I go to be with Jesus as this song beautifully said or would I go somewhere else. As I pondered these questions, I began searching for answers in my Bible and asking questions. My parents and I began visiting the church where my cousins attended.

Before coming to know Jesus, I was without hope and was a very timid child. As I began hearing the gospel preached, I knew my need for Jesus and I knew that I was a sinner in need of salvation. On March 20, 2011, I gave my life to Jesus and I still remember that day very vividly. I remember talking to the pastor of the church, Preacher Couch, and him taking me to a Sunday School room, reviewing the gospel with me, and leading me to Christ.

My life has been completely changed since that day. I no am no longer without hope of where I will be for eternity. I now have hope that Jesus is the Redeemer of my soul and I will be spending my eternity worshiping Him. I am no longer as timid as I once was and even though I'm still a bit of an introvert, I am eager to share about

Jesus and all He's done in my life. Since coming to know Jesus, I have substantially grown in my faith, found my passion in serving the local church, attended a Christian university, and felt God calling me to ministry. In obedience, I attended seminary and now have a degree in Christian Studies, and it is all because of Jesus.

Every testimony is significant and can be used by God to lead others to Him. Whenever you have the opportunity to share your story, I want to encourage you to share it with others because you never know who may need to hear it.

Conclusion

Salvation is a crucial point in the life of a believer. It is our root, the foundation for our faith. It is at the moment of our conversion where we are truly set free from the bondage of sin and restored back to God by placing our faith in the crucified and resurrected Savior. Through believing, confessing, and repenting, we are justified by the grace of God (Ephesians 2:8) and we are made into new creations in Christ (2 Corinthians 5:17). The day of our conversion is only the beginning of our discipleship journey, not the end (not even close).

CHAPTER 1 REFLECTION QUESTIONS

1. Why are we all in need of God's salvation?

2. In this chapter, we discussed that everyone's testimony is unique and powerful when sharing the gospel with others. Think of your own testimony for just a moment. How would you explain to someone your testimony in several sentences?

3. Is there anyone in your life that needs to hear the gospel of Jesus and your testimony? If so, plan to make time this week to reach out to them with the intention of sharing your faith.

Part Two
Sanctification

We Are Being Saved

In the last section, we examined the root of our faith, which was our conversion to Christ through salvation. This one-time event entered us into a relationship that will last through all eternity. In this section, we will examine the next portion of our journey through what we call sanctification. Sanctification sounds like a big, fancy theological word, but it simply means the process of becoming holy. Our journey as a Christian doesn't end at our conversion, rather it is simply the beginning and sanctification is the ongoing process of our holiness. The goal of the Christian life is to glorify God and become more like Christ each day.

Scripture has a lot to say about sanctification as well. Peter describes believers as "a chosen generation, a royal priesthood, a holy nation, His own special people, that you may proclaim the praises of Him who called you out of darkness into His marvelous light" (1 Peter 2:9). We are God's chosen people who are called to give Him praise and glory. But the problem, as we saw in the previous chapter, is that we are sinners saved by grace. Because of this, we cannot fulfill the command to "be holy, for [God is] holy" (see Leviticus 19:2 and 1 Peter 1:16). We are not perfect by no means, but with the help of the Holy Spirit, we are being sanctified daily (see 1 Peter 1:2). Our holiness will not be perfected until we are in heaven with Christ Himself (as we will see in part 3), but our goal each day should be to strive for holiness so that others may see Christ in us.

Sanctification is not something that can be accomplished in a single day; rather, it takes a lifetime of growing and learning each and every day. As we go about our analogy of a tree/plant, this portion will be considered the growth and nourishment we must go through as believers as we seek to be more like Jesus. This process begins the day of our conversion and lasts all the way through the moment we stand before Christ face to face, either through death or His second coming. The following chapters will give us an idea of how we can grow in our faith and become more like Jesus each day. Some are disciplines we must work on, while others are lifestyles we should strive to attain.

I hope the following topics challenge you and encourage you in becoming more like Christ as you strive to pursue holiness so that others may see Jesus in you.

2
GROWING THROUGH THE WORD

I currently work in a library at a local elementary school as a media clerk. My job consists of checking in and checking out books to students and helping them find books that interest them. Sometimes students are so eager for a certain book that they will put it "on hold" if it is already checked out to another student and they will patiently wait for it to get checked in. One of the highlights of my day is when a student comes back to the library the following day or week asking for that book they put on hold, and I get to see their face light up with excitement as I reach for the book on the cart behind my chair. They give a big thank you, sometimes even a hug, and a huge smile comes across their face as they walk out the library doors. As I watch these kids on a daily basis get excited over the next *Dog Man* book or whatever book makes them excited and eager to read, I can't help but wonder how much more excited we should be to pick up the Bible and read the living Word of God. The Bible is the most important book we will ever read in our lives. It's the only book that has the power to transform lives.

In order to grow in our relationship with God and become a better disciple, we must know who He is and the only way we can know His attributes is through His Word. As Christians we believe that the Bible is inerrant and infallible (meaning it is without error and trustworthy).

We also believe that the Bible is God's own words to us. Though it was written by human hands, God used them with the help of the Holy Spirit to write His redemptive story, so that we may know His amazing love for us. It's not just a book that was written thousands of years ago and has no significance to the modern reader. No, it's a book that transforms lives through the power of the Holy Spirit.

The writer of Hebrews even acknowledged this stating, "For the word of God is living and powerful, and sharper than any two-edged sword, piercing even to the division of soul and spirit, and of joints and marrow, and is a discerner of the thoughts and intents of the heart" (Hebrews 4:12). The Bible is living and powerful because it reveals to us God's own heart and love towards us who are wretched sinners undeserving of such grace and mercy. And though reading the Bible itself doesn't save us, it sustains us in our times of both joy and sorrow, it nourishes us as we hunger and thirst for the truth, and it encourages us as we seek to become more like Christ.

Bible Basics

Let's take a quick look at some Bible basics. Sometimes picking up the Bible and trying to read it can be intimidating. I remember getting my first Bible and looking through it not knowing where to start or how to read it, but as I grew in my faith, it became more natural. So if you've been a Christian for a while you may find this section kind of boring, but I feel it is necessary that we take a quick glimpse of how the Bible is laid out and how to read it. The Bible is made up of 66 books (39 in the Old Testament and 27 in the New Testament) and was originally written in three languages: (1) Hebrew, (2) Aramaic, and (3) Greek. There are different types of genres found within these books. For example, the first two books of the Bible, Genesis and Exodus, would be considered historical books because Moses gives his audience a detailed account of the beginning of time as well as his own life through the Hebrews' enslavement in Egypt. Along with historical genre, there is also law, poetry, wisdom, and prophecy that are all found within the Old Testament.

In the New Testament, the genres include (1) narratives in the four gospel accounts as the writers tell about Jesus' life and ministry, (2) the history of the early church in Acts, (3) epistles written by the apostles, and (4) apocalyptic in the book of Revelation. Though each book may have a different genre and a different human author, there's no doubt that the Bible is coherent from Genesis to Revelation with this as the central message: God's love for sinners is so infinite that He sent His Son to redeem, reconcile, and restore all who believe so that they too may live and worship in His glory forever, just how He had intended.

Now let's take a minute to look at how the books of the Bible are laid out. If you're a new Christian this can be tricky to navigate, and if you're a mature believer who's been reading and studying the Bible for quite some time, please bear with me for just a moment. Each book of the Bible is broken down by chapters and then by verses. For example 2 Peter has three chapters and chapter two contains 22 verses. Another example I would like to use is the book of Psalms, because it has so many chapters. The Psalms have 150 chapters and chapter 119 has (get this) 176 verses in it making it the longest chapter in the Bible! What I love so much about Psalm 119 is that the whole chapter is a Hebrew acrostic dedicated to the Word of God (or the law of God). While books of the Bible are broken up by chapters and verses, it is important to remember that when reading Scripture, we must not pick and choose the verses that sound good; rather, we must read it in its entire context.

I've heard an analogy about how to read books of the Bible in this way. Think about someone writing you a letter. Would you just choose one line from that letter and meditate on that only? Of course not! You would read the letter in its entirety to understand the context to which the letter was written in. When we do that, we not only understand the context, but we understand the intention of the author as well. It's the same thing with the Bible. While not all books are written as letters like the epistles are, each book contains stories that are meant to be read in their entirety to understand the context and the author's intended purpose for writing the book. Now, I'm not saying you must read the entire Bible cover to cover over the course of a year to understand the full context of Scripture. While it is a good goal to have and I would encourage you to read the Bible from beginning to end at some point in your life, just take time and dive in deep to what God has revealed to us through His Word. Take one chapter a day and meditate on what God is revealing to you, take your time and don't rush through it. The beauty of the Bible is that it is living and active through the help of the Holy Spirit, who illuminates our hearts and minds to the truths God reveals to us through His Word.

Why is Reading the Bible So Important?

After examining the basics of the Bible, I'm hoping that you are seeing why we should take our Bible reading so seriously. As mentioned before, it's not merely another book to read, rather it is the living Word of God, His very words penned down so that we may know His heart. Daily Bible reading helps us in our journey in effective discipleship. Once we become believers, one of the desires of our hearts is that we want to become more like Jesus. In order to become more like Jesus, we must first know who He is. And in order to know who He is, we must read the Bible. The Bible is filled with countless stories of God's love for people and tells of all His amazing attributes.

When we read the Bible, we are reading the very heart of God. Every word printed in the Bible is breathed out by God (2 Timothy 3:16), making Scripture authoritative, accurate, and holy. In his second letter to Timothy, Paul writes that because Scripture is breathed out by God, it is also "profitable for doctrine, for reproof, for correction, for instruction in righteousness," (2 Timothy 3:16) that we may be "thoroughly equipped for every good work" (2 Timothy 3:17). This is why the Bible is so crucial to our growth as a believer, because everything in it is from God and it is how He chose to reveal Himself to us.

In seminary, one of the many things I learned is that God reveals Himself to us in two ways. The first way is through what is referred to as general revelation. General revelation is God's way of revealing Himself to us through natural means such as seeing a beautiful sunrise. Through these natural means, He is ultimately revealing Himself as

Creator of the universe. Paul even writes this in Romans 1, "For since the creation of the world His invisible attributes are clearly seen, being understood by the things that are made, even His eternal power and Godhead, so that they are without excuse, because, although they knew God, they did not glorify Him as God, nor were thankful, but became futile in their thoughts, and their foolish hearts were darkened" (Romans 1:20-21). What Paul is getting at here in this passage is that mankind had no reason or excuse to turn against God as He did reveal Himself to them, but mankind rebelled anyway. General revelation reveals to people everywhere that there indeed is a God, even if they do not believe.

The next way God reveals Himself is through what is called special revelation. In special revelation, God reveals Himself through the Bible and through the incarnation of His Son, Jesus, who is the visible image of the invisible God (Colossians 1:15). While general revelation reveals to this world that God does exist, there is no personal knowledge of who God is. Special revelation, on the other hand, is more personal in that God's words through Scripture take up room in our hearts and minds, which can lead us to a relationship with our Creator. Nature cannot reveal to us how Jesus came to die on the cross for our sins, but the Bible does and it is through reading and studying God's Word that we can truly know the Way to salvation. Special revelation, with the power of the Holy Spirit, leads us to salvation. This is why Scripture is so very important to our faith and sanctification. Our Bible intake should continue throughout our lives as believers because in His Holy Word, we find how we are to live and grow as disciples of Christ.

Pitfalls to Avoid

Bible reading is crucial to our growth, but we need to be aware of some pitfalls to avoid. The first pitfall is making the Bible about us. Contrary to popular belief, the Bible is not about us, it's about God and His glory. As we read and study the Scriptures, let's be careful to not make the passage about us and instead focus on the attributes of God, giving glory to Him. Now I'm not saying we shouldn't examine our hearts as we read the Bible, but we need to be careful not to place ourselves in the story that was intended to put God's glory on display. Let me give you a quick example. If we choose to read and study the popular story of David and Goliath, the main idea is that David believed God could defeat Goliath and he put his faith and trust in the LORD to do so. The main idea would not be that we are David and the circumstances we face are Goliath and we need God to defeat the Goliath standing in front of us. While that sounds like a good analogy, it is not the intended message of the original author. The original message of that story was to highlight God's victory and glory. As we seek to study Scripture for ourselves, we need to be aware of such pitfalls.

Another pitfall that needs to be addressed is this one: "What does this passage mean to me?" While this sounds like an innocent question, the 'to me' part of it can be detrimental in our studies of the Scripture as it implies that what that passage means to you may be different than what it means to me. Though Scripture is open to many different interpretations, there's also a unity to the message the Bible is communicating as a whole. That is why it is important to read within the context of Scripture and use the application portion of your study to see how you can apply that passage in your own life. This will be discussed more in the next section with some helpful Bible study methods.

Lastly, don't make your Bible reading merely something to check off a list. This is one pitfall that I struggle with frequently. It's great to set goals and use plans when reading the Bible, but we need to be careful to not make our time in the Word something we check off our daily to-do list and not think about what we've read throughout our day; rather, our ultimate goal in Scripture reading is to draw nearer to God, meditating on His Word, and remembering His promises. When we make our daily Bible reading a legalistic task, we are prone to missing out on hearing His voice as we read His precious Word. While God desires for us to read and study His Word, He doesn't want us to read just to be reading it, rather He wants us to read with intentionality and a desire to grow in our faith that we may become more like Him. The only way we can truly know the heart of God is by faithfully reading the Word He has revealed to us and applying its truths to our own lives.

Bible Study Methods

There are many different methods you can use while studying the Bible and this is not an exhaustive list, but I want to use this section to highlight a few that may be useful to you as you pursue a deeper relationship with the Father. These are merely aids to help in your personal Bible studies and there is no right or wrong way of doing these. They are just suggestions to encourage as you dive into Scripture.

1. Methods that contain acronyms

One method that I have grown familiar with over the last few years has been the HEAR method, originally written by Robby and Kandi Gallaty. The acronym HEAR stands for Highlight, Explain, Apply, Respond. At my church, we have used this method in our youth discipleship groups to help them seek and understand the Scriptures better. Each week, students were encouraged to read the Bible chapters for each day of the week and use the HEAR method as written in the *Foundations* workbook that was provided to them. The HEAR method in the *Foundations* book is as follows:

- Highlight the verses that speak to you (this could be simply writing out the name of the book or the chapters/verses that stood out to you).
- Explain what the passage means (this could be who was the original author/audience or what was the Holy Spirit's originally trying to communicate).
- Apply what God is saying in these verses to your life (this could be how you can apply the message to your own life or how does it apply today).
- Respond to what you've read (this would be where you see a call to action or writing a prayer to how you feel God is calling you to respond).[4]

This method works well if you like having an outline to follow and an easy acronym to remember.

2. Studying one book of the Bible at a time

Another method that may be helpful to you is to study one book of the Bible at a time. This may be intimidating if you're new to this, but try picking a book of the Bible that you would like to study and go in depth with it. An easy one to start with is the Gospel of Mark because it is a short narrative about the life of Jesus. Any of the Gospels would be easy to pick up and read due to their narrative genre. In the Old Testament, an easy book with a few chapters to read is Ruth, which is also a narrative. Start off with books that are easier to read and understand rather than a book like Leviticus that is filled with Old Testament law, which can be difficult to understand. This will make Bible reading more enjoyable and not feel like a chore. Of course, all Scripture is important and is worth reading and studying, but as you begin your journey in Bible reading, don't overwhelm yourself. Instead, choose a book and dig deep into its content and seek to understand the heart of God.

3. Scripture memorization

The next method that may help in your Bible intake is memorizing Scripture. I learned the importance of this method during my time in college and seminary. The author of Psalm 119 writes in verse 11 that he has hidden God's Word in his heart that he may not sin against Him. The author here makes a point to remind us that memorizing Scripture and hiding it in our hearts is very important in our Christian walk. When we hide God's Word in our hearts, we are able to pull it out when we need encouragement on a bad day, a good day or we may even need it when we find ourselves in the midst of temptation. Jesus even found Himself in this situation as He was tempted by the devil in the wilderness.

According to Matthew 4, Jesus was led into the wilderness to be tempted after fasting for forty days and forty nights. The devil knew Jesus was hungry and tempted Him to turn the stones into bread. Jesus then answers Satan, "It is written, 'Man shall not live by bread alone, but by every word that proceeds from the mouth of God.'" (Matthew 4:4). Next, the devil takes Jesus to the highest point of the city and says, "If You are the Son of God, throw Yourself down. For it is written: 'He shall give His angels charge over you,' and, 'In their hands they shall bear you up, lest you dash your foot against a stone.'" (Matthew 4:6). Jesus responds with, "It is written again, 'You shall not tempt the LORD your God.'" (Matthew 4:7). The last way Satan tempts Jesus is by showing Him all the kingdoms of the world and offering it all to him if Jesus would bow down and worship Satan. Jesus again responds, "Away with you, Satan! For it is written, 'You shall worship the LORD your God, and Him only you shall serve.'" (Matthew 4:10). And at that moment Satan left and the angels tended to their Lord.

We see through this story just how important it is to memorize Scripture, because we realize that Satan even knows Scripture. However, instead of using the Scriptures in the right context, Satan twists it. Just as Satan asked Eve in the Garden of Eden, "Has God indeed said...?" (see Genesis 3:1), Satan does the same even today.

We must memorize Scripture, read it in context, and store it up in our hearts and minds that it may be used as a defense against the enemy. The Apostle Paul describes the Word of God as the sword of the Spirit in the armor of God passage found in Ephesians 6. The Word must be our weapon of defense and offense as our souls endure spiritual warfare against the enemy.

Practical Steps to Making Bible Intake a Habit

Reading the Bible isn't something that comes naturally for many of us. While our desire to grow in the Word becomes stronger after we receive salvation, sometimes we need a practical plan put in place to keep us in the Word on a daily basis. That is often why Bible intake is considered to be a spiritual discipline because it is something we have to work at and cultivate in our lives. Donald Whitney wrote an entire book on this matter entitled *Spiritual Disciplines for the Christian Life,* and it is one I highly recommend if you are interested in learning more about these disciplines in depth. Whitney explains the goal of spiritual discipline is ultimately godliness. He reiterates to his readers that when we remember the goal of spiritual disciplines is godliness, then practicing these disciplines becomes a delight rather than drudgery.[5] I love thinking about it that way. When we remember that spiritual disciplines like Bible reading, praying, serving, etc. are not merely something we check off our to-do list but rather think of them as ways in which we grow in godliness to become more like Jesus, then our outlook should be that of delight. God has provided ways for us to grow in grace and knowledge, and we must not take that for granted.

Now that we've seen that reading the Bible should be our delight as it helps us grow in godliness, let's look at a few practical ways that can help us make Bible intake a habit. The following list is not a checklist you must follow in order to get the most out of your Bible reading, rather they are only suggestions to help guide you as you do read. Everyone has different things that work for them, and I realize some of these may not work for every person and that's okay. They have helped me set structure in my quiet time and it may work for you as well.

1. Create a goal: I'm a goal setter. I always have been and I probably always will be. I like knowing that when I set a goal, I can achieve it which makes me feel accomplished. It also helps me in my Bible reading because I know I have a timeline to work with. I've always had the desire to read the entire Bible in a year and several years ago I made it my goal to do so. I found a plan online where I would need to read 2-3 chapters per day in order to achieve the goal and I was determined to do it. A year had passed and by God's grace, I can say that I did achieve my goal of reading the entire Bible in a year. I learned so much that year about God's love, grace, and mercy as I read His redemptive story in its entirety. My point here is that I set a goal for myself that I would read God's Word each day through a plan I wanted to follow and by God's grace, I achieved it.

   When we set goals for ourselves in Bible reading, it gives us a timeline to which we can ultimately achieve. Maybe your goal is to memorize one Scripture per day, maybe it's to read one book of the Bible in a week or a month, maybe it's to read the whole Bible in a year or three years. There is no goal too big or too small when it comes to Bible intake. As long as you are reading the Bible with the ultimate goal of pursuing godliness, as Whitney mentioned, then you are on the right track.

2. Set a time of day to read: Another practical way that may help us in our pursuit of daily Bible intake is setting a time of day to read. When Christians set a certain time of the day to read their Bible, they usually call it their quiet time as they steady their hearts and minds before the Lord. In this section, I'll refer to our time in the Word as our quiet time. Most people I know and have talked to about this usually set their quiet time in the morning hours to ensure their day is starting off right. For me, it depends, which is why this section is one I personally need to work on.

During the summer months, it's easy for me to start my morning off with Bible reading. I don't have anywhere to be and can take all the time I need to dive into Scripture. During the school months, which is when I work and wake up at 5 a.m. everyday, is a completely different story. I'm not a morning person at all, never have been and probably never will be. When I wake up at 5 a.m., my brain isn't fully functioning. I need to wake up first and drink my coffee, then by the time I'm fully awake and functioning, it's time to get ready, get dressed, eat breakfast, and leave for work. Oftentimes, I read my quiet time when I get home from work and just do a quick devotion on a Bible app first thing in the morning. For you it may be different.

You may be a morning person ready to hit the ground running as soon as you wake up. Or, you may be like me who isn't a morning person and would prefer to do your quiet time in the afternoon. The amazing thing is there is no set time that you must read the Bible, that is something you must do on your own. Whether you set your time in the morning or the evening, or whether you set aside five minutes or one hour to read your Bible, don't compare how your quiet time is to others because theirs may look different than yours and that's okay. The goal here in Bible intake is that you are striving to understand the heart of God and you're doing so not out of obligation, but out of a delightful heart.

3. Be engaged as you read: This step is one that has helped me immensely in my daily Bible reading. I am a visual learner, meaning I need to see how things are done in order to understand it. Just reading it doesn't help me, I need to visualize what it is I'm reading. Once I realized this, I made sure I was engaged with what I was reading in the Bible. Whether it was highlighting or underlining key passages, journaling about it, or being creative and drawing a picture to help me visualize a passage, these things have helped me to better understand Scripture. Maybe you're similar to me and need to have a creative outlet in order to get the most of your Bible reading. I want to encourage you to find ways for you that will help you stay engaged in the Bible as you read and study.

4. Pray through the passage: Prayer is an essential part of our daily life. It's our direct source to communicate with the Father. The most beautiful thing about Scripture is that it is God's very words to us so why not use them to pray back to the Lord. As you go through Scripture, you may read a passage that glorifies God and want to pray those words back to Him in adoration. Or you may read a passage that speaks to a sin you've been struggling with in your life and you want to pray that Scripture to God with a heart of confession and remorse. For example, you may be reading Psalm 139 and you reach verses 23-24 which reads, "Search me, O God, and know my heart; test me and know my anxious thoughts. See if there is any offensive way in me, and lead me in the way everlasting" (NIV). These words you may want to pray when you are struggling with a sin that you are trying to break free from. With a humble heart, come before the Lord in prayer and praise Him using Scripture as your guide.

5. Show yourself grace: All of the steps above have shown you practical ways in which you can make Bible reading a habit, but this step is also crucial. Don't be afraid to show yourself grace. There will be days when you forget to read and study Scripture. There will be days when you don't feel like it. Or there may be seasons in your life where you go through a dry spell in your Christian walk.

I've recently had one of these and I can tell you it is not comforting being away from the Word for a length of time, but I've found that while I may beat myself over not reading my Bible, God always meets me where I am and shows up with immeasurable grace. He's taught me through these dry seasons that I need to show myself grace as He has shown me grace. I'm not perfect, nor will I ever be in this life and He knows that full well. All I need to do is pray and seek His face, asking to place the desire to study His word with joy back into my heart and He will do so. As you go about your days in pursuit of godliness, don't be afraid to show yourself grace for there will be days when you forget or won't feel like doing your daily Bible reading. God is always there with open arms, ready to take you in, and give you desires to become more like Jesus.

Conclusion

Through this chapter, we have seen the importance of Bible reading, methods to which we can read the Bible, and practical steps we can take in making Bible intake a daily habit. As we go about our daily lives, may we seek to become diligent in reading the precious Word of God. The Word that is eternal (Psalm 119:89) and is flawless (Psalm 18:30). May we read the Bible with true adoration and excitement as the kids at school do over the latest *Dog Man* graphic novel. Unlike a novel though, the words of the Bible are sacred and holy, worthy of meditating on and hiding them deep within our hearts. I pray that as you seek to become more like Jesus, you will see the beauty and value the words of the Bible has to offer and that you may never take those words for granted.

CHAPTER 2 REFLECTION QUESTIONS

1. Why is reading the Bible so important to our growth as believers?

2. What does your daily Bible intake (or quiet time) look like? If you don't have a daily quiet time, what can you start doing to make it into a habit?

3. What does your plan of action for reading the Bible this week look like? List out which verses or books of the Bible you are going to read and meditate on this week.

3
Growing Through Community

I'm what you may consider an extroverted introvert. I know, crazy right? Let me explain. I enjoy being around people, but sometimes I need my space and want to be left alone. It's quite funny actually because I started realizing this while I was an intern at my church a few years ago. I was a youth ministry intern at my home church for about a year. During that time, I was busy helping plan and execute Wednesday night games and youth events. While I enjoyed youth ministry and gained practical ministry experience, I also realized that being my extroverted self was draining for me. I would go home after a Wednesday night service and feel mentally exhausted because I had to be extroverted for an hour or two as I prepped for games and helped make sure everything ran smoothly. Even though I was exhausted by the end of the evening, I wouldn't trade it for anything, because it was during that time where I made sweet connections with the teenage girls and we would talk about important things like life and faith.

I say all that because even though my natural tendency was to be introverted, I was aware of the importance of solid community and knew our youth needed someone to look up to. We're not meant to do the Christian life alone. Whether we're extroverted or introverted by nature, God innately put the desire for community in each of our hearts. So in this chapter, we are going to dive into how community helps us grow in our discipleship journey.

Community within the Trinity

Community is found all throughout the Bible, but the greatest and most essential form of community is found in God Himself. God represents the perfect form of community through what we refer to as the Trinity, one Holy God in three distinct Persons. The Trinity consists of God the Father, God the Son, and God the Holy Spirit. The doctrine of the Trinity can be quite confusing and may be something we will never fully grasp until we are glorified in heaven, but it is still an important doctrine to our faith. God has been in community with Himself through the Trinity since the beginning of time. In fact, we see the Trinity in community in the creation account found in Genesis. In Genesis 1:26 God says, "Let *Us* make man in *Our* image, according to *Our* likeness" (*emphasis mine*). This verse communicates to us that God indeed is a Triune God who has been in existence for all eternity. Michael F. Bird defines the Trinity's roles in creation in this way, "the Father is the grounds of creation…the Son is the principle of creation….[and] the Spirit is the divine power in creation."[6] Each Person of the Trinity had a distinct role in the creation account as they still do in this present age.

Not only do we see the Trinity present in the creation account, but we also see the Trinity communing at Jesus' baptism. Matthew writes the following in his gospel account, "When He had been baptized, Jesus came up immediately from the water; and behold, the heavens were opened to Him, and He saw the Spirit of God descending like a dove and alighting upon Him. And suddenly a voice came from heaven, saying, "This is My beloved Son, in whom I am well pleased" (Matthew 3:16-17). Here we see God the Son in the flesh being baptized, the Holy Spirit descending down like a dove, and the Father speaking boldly of His love for His Son. This story always amazes me because we get a representation of each Person in the Trinity all at once.

All throughout Scripture we see the significance of the Triune God and how important it is on our view of community. In his article on community, J. Strukova writes about how "an evangelically based view of community is grounded essentially in the transformative work of the Triune God."[7] It is only through the love of the Father, the sacrifice of the Son, and the conviction and help of the Holy Spirit that we too can have community with the Triune God.

Community with God

So far we've discussed God in community with Himself, now we're going to look at how we have community with God. As we saw in chapter one, God created men and women to be in a perfect community with Him from the start. Before Adam and Eve sinned, everything was perfect and they were living in the very presence of God. This was the way God intended it to be. However, after Adam and Eve had sinned, the community they once experienced with God and with one another was now broken. Every person who has come after Adam and Eve now has to live with the consequences of sin and; therefore, are separated from God until one decides to place his or her faith in Christ Jesus. Upon making our profession of faith as discussed in chapter one, we now are reconciled back to God in a right relationship with Him. Through our salvation, our community with God has been restored, because of the precious blood of Jesus. So how then are we to commune with God?

1. Through Prayer

The first way we can have community with our God is through prayer. Prayer is simply talking to God and sharing with Him all the burdens, joys, and questions that are on your heart. Prayer is our direct access to the Father and something that shouldn't be taken lightly. When we ask for things in prayer, may we not view God as a genie who grants every wish we command. Rather, as we pray, may our hearts be humbled and attuned to God as Jesus' model prayer teaches us in Matthew 6. The prayer reads, "Our Father in heaven, hallowed be your name, your kingdom come, your will be done on earth as it is in heaven. Give us today our daily bread. Forgive us our debts, as we also have forgiven our debtors. And lead us not into temptation, but deliver us from the evil one" (Matthew 6:9-13, NIV).

Through this model prayer, we see that God is glorified in both the beginning and end of the prayer. In the middle, we see that even though things are being asked of God (like provision and forgiveness), they are being asked in accordance to His will and His way. It's important to remember that when we pray, we are not merely asking for things, but we are trying to be more in tune with God Himself. Just like a conversation between two friends, prayer is a conversation between you and God. Sometimes we're the one doing the talking and sometimes we're the one sitting still and doing the listening. Do we hear an audible voice from God? No, but sometimes we can hear His still, small voice through solitude and Scripture reading. Which leads me to my next point.

2. Through Bible Intake

As we saw in the previous chapter, reading Scripture is essential in our growth as a Christian. It is also essential as we seek to have a relationship with God. To read the Bible is to know the very heart of God. Bible reading helps us to grow in community with God because we are reading and studying His very words. Throughout the Bible, we see God's attributes of love, grace, mercy, and holiness fill the pages. We also see that because He is holy and we are not, He does have righteous anger towards sin that needs to be dealt with. Praise God that He sent Jesus to take on our sin debt that we could have never paid on our own. As we seek the Lord in His Word, He will reveal to us things about ourselves that we won't like and convict us of sins that we need to repent of. Use your Bible reading time as an act of worship unto the Lord and allow the Holy Spirit to work within you as you study and read about the Holy Triune God.

3. Through Worship

Another way we can experience community with God is through worship. According to the Merriam-Webster dictionary, worship is a verb and is defined as "to regard with great or extravagant respect, honor, or devotion."[8] We were designed by God to be worshipers. God created each and every one of us with the ability to worship and while that is a beautiful thing, sometimes we may find ourselves worshiping something or someone else other than God due to our sin nature. This is why God put in the Ten Commandments that we are not to have any gods before Him and we are not to have any graven images (see Exodus 20:3-4). Due to our sin nature, God knew we would have trouble in worshiping false idols and rightly so. At some point, we have all struggled with this in one way or another. The Bible tells us, however, that we are to worship God only as He is worthy of all our adoration and praise (see Psalm 103:1, Psalm 150:6; 1 Chronicles 16:23-27).

When we worship the Lord, we must do so as Jesus proclaims in John 4:23-24: to worship in spirit and in truth. When we worship in this manner, our worship is not in vain; rather, it is genuine and glorifying to God. How do we worship the Lord in spirit and in truth? To worship in spirit and in truth, our posture must be humble and our minds must be focused fully on the One we are worshiping.

Worship is not merely an experience that we witness once or twice a week during church (though that is important). Worship, rather, is an integral part of a believer's daily life. Paul states in Romans 12:1 that we are to be living sacrifices unto the Lord, meaning everything we do should be an act of worship to God. Paul even states in 1 Corinthians 10:31 that "whether you eat or drink, or whatever you do, do all to the glory of God." Worshiping the Lord should be central in every aspect of our life, whether we're at home relaxing with family, working at our jobs, or even going to the grocery store. Our lives should be marked by the love, admiration, and praise we have for King Jesus.

Through growing in our community with God, we grow in knowing ourselves better. In light of the perfection of Jesus, we see ourselves as imperfect sinners in need of daily grace and mercy. Through daily prayer, Bible intake, and worship we should strive each day to become more Christlike both in word and deed.

Community with Others

While community with God is the most important thing to have, He also calls us to have community with other believers to help strengthen us in our Christian walk. This is why being an active member of a local church is so important to our faith. When we gather at church each Sunday morning, we are participating in a community as God intended us to be in. God doesn't just want us to go to church, sit in a pew, listen to a sermon, and leave. He wants us to build relationships with fellow believers, which is why most churches offer weekly groups, such as Sunday School and small groups. It is through groups like these where we find the most opportunity to do life with others and live out biblical community. It's through these programs where we encourage and build up one another (1 Thessalonians 5:11), bear with each other and forgive (Colossians 3:13), carry each other's burdens (Galatians 6:2), confess sins and pray for one another (James 5:16), and share things that the Lord has been teaching us in our lives. Through these things, we see a picture of how the body of Christ is supposed to work and operate.

Though we all have different personalities, traits, and gifts, we are all co-laborers for the gospel of Christ (1 Corinthians 3:9). If you are not actively involved in a church or small group, I want to encourage you to find one where you can be open and honest about your faith and personal life. Personally, being a part of my church has been absolutely amazing and life changing, knowing I can openly share about anything that's going on in my life. If I have amazing news, I know my church family will rejoice right alongside me. If I have tough news and need prayer, I know they will grieve alongside me and lift me up in prayer as I would do the same for them. The amazing thing about church and fellowship with other believers is that we don't have to do life alone. We have those who love the Lord around us, praying for us, and encouraging us every step of the way.

We see in Scripture what biblical community looks like through the early church. Acts 2 shows us the growth of the early church and how it operated. Believers in the early church had all things in common, and in an act of obedience they sold their possessions to provide for those around them (see Acts 2:44-45). The next few verses show us how the early church met and operated. Acts 2:46-47 reads, "So continuing daily with one accord in the temple, and breaking bread from house to house, they ate their food with gladness and simplicity of heart, praising God and having favor with all the people. And the Lord added to the church daily those who were being saved." We see that they met in the temple and partook in the Lord's Supper at each other's homes, but above all they praised God and He added to His church daily.

In the early church, we see an emphasis placed on community as believers met with one another in homes and at the temple. God clearly views community within the local body as something to be a regular aspect of a believer's life. We were not made to do life alone; rather, we were made for community and to build strong, lasting relationships with others. We may not have the same interests, hobbies, or musical tastes as some of our brothers and sisters in Christ, but that doesn't matter. We all share one commonality that holds us all together, and that is our saving faith in Jesus. How wonderful is that!

Growing in Discipleship through Mentoring

Along with building community from within our church, another way to grow in our discipleship is through mentoring. Chuck Lawless defines mentoring as, "A God-given relationship in which one growing Christian encourages and equips another believer to reach his or her potential as a disciple of Christ."[9] By this definition, we are either the mentor or the mentee as Lawless explains throughout his book. Christian mentoring generally involves two people: (1) the mentor who is more mature in the faith and eager to teach and share biblical truths and (2) the mentee who is growing in their faith and eager to learn under someone of more wisdom. When we engage in mentoring, we either take on the role of the mentor or the mentee. Essentially we can be either one because there is always going to be someone older than us who we can look up to and there is always going to be someone younger than us searching for such a role model.

The Apostle Paul gives us a glimpse at what this kind of discipleship looks like in Titus 2. In this passage, Paul is charging Titus, an early church leader, to "teach the older men to be temperate, worthy of respect, self-controlled, and sound in faith, in love and in endurance," (Titus 2:2, NIV) and to also "teach the older women to be reverent in the way they live, not to be slanderers or addicted to much wine, but to teach what is good." (Titus 2:3, NIV) However, Titus is not the only one responsible for discipling the men and women of his church.

If we keep reading, Paul goes on to say that as the older men and women are being discipled and mentored, they too should disciple and mentor the younger men and women of the church. Paul mentions that the older women should encourage the younger women to love their husbands and children, to be kind, and to be self-controlled, just to name a few (see Titus 2:4-5). The older men have the same task, setting a good example for the younger men and encouraging them in being self-controlled (see Titus 2:6-8).

As we engage in the role of either being a mentor or a mentee, let's look to this example in Titus 2. If you are the mentor, strive to set a good example to your mentee. Though none of us are perfect, let's do our very best to demonstrate what it means to be a genuine follower of Jesus. If you are a mentee, heed the knowledge and the wisdom of your mentor. More than likely your mentor is more mature than you either physically or spiritually or both. Listen to what they have to say and soak it all in, because it is very likely that the wisdom they share with you will be needed in the future.

I learned the importance of mentorship during both my junior and senior years of college when I served as a chaplain and an intern respectively. I saw the Titus 2 model of mentorship play out right before my eyes. As a chaplain, I was responsible for ministering to and discipling commuter girls. My job was to pour out into them and I would be poured into by the small group of chaplains that would meet with their assigned intern. These were sweet times to minister to one another and lift each other up in prayer.

As an intern, not only did I pour into my chaplain girls, but I was also poured into by our chaplain coordinator who oversaw the entire chaplain program. She is such an amazing mentor who I look up to even to this day. Her wisdom has stuck with me even after graduating college and I still think of life applications she has taught me over the years. She has shown me what true mentorship looks like through the chaplain ministry, that we must be poured into and filled with truth in order to pour out into the lives of others and do it all out of love.

We saw that Titus 2 gave us a great example of what mentorship looks like, but the term mentorship is never mentioned specifically in the Bible. Though it isn't explicitly mentioned, the concept plays out in several places throughout Scripture. Let's take a brief look at a few.

First, let's look at the Old Testament in the book of Ruth. Here we see Ruth seek mentorship from her mother-in-law, Naomi. The first chapter of Ruth opens with Naomi losing her husband, Elimelek, and both her sons, one of whom is married to Ruth. With this news, Naomi heads back to her homeland and discourages her daughter-in-laws to come with her, but Ruth refuses and makes the famous statement,

"Where you go I will go, and where you stay I will stay. Your people will be my people and your God my God. Where you die I will die, and there I will be buried. May the LORD deal with me, be it ever so severely, if anything but death separates you and me" (Ruth 1:16-17, NIV). This statement is bold coming from a non-Jewish woman. Ruth, the Moabite, was so loyal to Naomi that she would convert and believe in God. Throughout the rest of the book, we see Naomi mentoring Ruth as Ruth finds herself a kinsman redeemer in Boaz. Naomi played an important role in Ruth's life as a mentor.

In the New Testament, we see two great examples of mentorship in the life of the Apostle Paul. In the first example, Paul is the one being mentored. After Paul's miraculous conversion on the Damascus Road, many of the disciples were skeptical of Paul because of his past. At first, when the apostles saw Paul they didn't see a converted, faithful follower of Jesus, rather they saw the man who murdered Christians and persecuted the church. Acts 9 tells us that many of them were afraid of Paul, except Barnabas who took Paul in and mentored him (see Acts 9:26-27). Throughout the beginning of the book of Acts, Barnabas and Paul formed a mentor/mentee relationship until they eventually went their separate ways as recorded in Acts 15.

In the second example, Paul is the one doing the mentoring to the young preacher, Timothy. In his mentoring, Paul is helping Timothy become better equipped in the ministry. Through the two letters written to Timothy, Paul guides and encourages Timothy in his spiritual walk. Paul, who was much more spiritually mature and had more experience in ministry, put forth the time and effort into mentoring Timothy who was shepherding a church of his own. Through these two distinct relationships, Paul gives us a picture of what it looks like to first be a mentee under someone who has more experience and then be a mentor to someone who needs spiritual guidance.

While the stories of Ruth and Naomi and Paul with Barnabas and Timothy are great examples of mentorship, perhaps the greatest example of mentorship in all of the Bible is Jesus with His twelve disciples. Jesus is the best mentor anyone could ever have. Can you imagine being one of the Twelve and hearing your Savior preach and teach right before your very eyes? I can imagine it was an amazing experience. The Twelve were mentees of the greatest Mentor to ever live, and what He taught them would be passed down from generation to generation because of their faithfulness to Him. We see many examples in the New Testament where He taught them how to live through parables and answering questions they may have had. Even through the Sermon on the Mount in Matthew 5-7, we find Him teaching the crowds and His disciples practical ways in which they can make the most out of their spiritual lives.

Just like the disciples, Christ is first and foremost our greatest Mentor and One we should be seeking in having a mentorship with. Only when we have a personal relationship with Christ, who is constantly pouring into us through His Holy Spirit, can we be effective mentors to others in our church and community. In order to do that, we must be actively abiding in Christ. In John 15, Jesus explains exactly what this means by stating, "Abide in Me, and I in you. As the branch cannot bear fruit of itself, unless it abides in the vine, neither can you, unless you abide in Me. 'I am the vine, you are the branches. He who abides in Me, and I in him, bears much fruit; for without Me you can do nothing'" (John 15:4-5). Without Christ, we are nothing and can do nothing apart from Him. At the moment of conversion, we begin our discipleship journey and from that point on, we are to abide in Him. We cannot be effective disciples or mentors if we are not abiding in Christ our Lord.

Conclusion

The Bible places a great emphasis on community. We were created for community with God and with others. Therefore, we must be intentional in how we are partaking in community. In our community with God, we need to have daily communication with Him through Bible reading and prayer. In our community with others, we need to be plugged into a local church body and even find a mentor or mentee to do life with. Through such communities, we are becoming more like Christ and growing in our faith.

CHAPTER 3 REFLECTION QUESTIONS

1. In this chapter, we see that being in community with God is essential in our Christian walk. How are you engaging in community with God currently?

2. Along with community with God, we see that we are made for community with others to help strengthen us in our discipleship journey. If you are currently a part of a local church, how has being a part of a community strengthened your walk with God? If you are not currently a part of a local church, I encourage you to look for a church where you can be actively involved and become a part of a strong Christian community.

3. In Titus 2, we see the example of older and younger believers taking part in mentoring. Who is someone you can be a mentor to and help them grow deeper in their faith?

4. Who is someone you can be a mentee to, who you can learn from and will help you grow deeper in your faith?

4
Growing Through Serving

In 1 Corinthians, Paul refers to all believers as the body of Christ (1 Corinthians 12:27). In these next two chapters, we are going to examine a few ways in which we act as the body of Christ through our churches and in the world around us. This chapter will focus on service and how it shapes us in our pursuit of growing in grace.

Why Do We Serve?

Serving doesn't come naturally to us, does it? As humans we have the tendency to be self-centered and sometimes even arrogant, so humbling ourselves to be able to serve Christ and others can be difficult. The world we live in tells us that we need to be served rather than serving in order to have the best life by the world's standards. This is why the Kingdom of Christ is not like the kingdoms this world has to offer and was not the kingdom Israel expected as the people longed for their promised Messiah in the Old Testament. Israel was expecting a conquering King who would ride into battle and destroy the Roman empire. However, their promised King was actually a lowly servant born in a manger, riding on a donkey on Palm Sunday, washing His disciples feet, and ultimately dying the most gruesome and embarrassing death by taking on the world's sins on the cross. Nobody else in all of history has ever made such a sacrifice and Christ calls us as

His disciples to live in this servanthood mindset that others will see and know Him for who He truly is. But we cannot do it on our own. Thankfully we have the Holy Spirit living inside of us, giving us the desire and willingness to serve others.

When we serve others, not only are we making someone's life a little easier, but we are also reflecting Jesus' character. As we continue on in this chapter, let's place our focus on the ultimate goal which is to serve God and through serving God, our desire should be to serve others. Serving is an act of self-sacrifice because we are giving up something we may want in order to bless others around us.

I witnessed a great example of humble service within our student ministry last summer when we went to FUGE camp. During our week there, I saw our students grow in their desire to serve, and one afternoon the FUGE staff had a need to set up for an event later that evening. Our group volunteered to help set up and tear down the layout and decorations for this event during what was supposed to be their free time. Students eagerly moved and stacked chairs, blew up balloons, and did whatever else the FUGE staff needed. It touched my heart seeing teenagers willingly give up a bit of their free time to show the love of Christ through their actions. We too need to have that same willingness to serve as I saw our students do that night and put serving into practice in our daily lives. Although it may seem difficult to do so, we do have the most perfect example of servanthood through our Savior.

Our Perfect Example

Though serving does not come naturally to us, there is One who exemplified the action of serving in His daily life and His name is Jesus. He did not struggle to serve because it was in His nature and His purpose to do so. In Matthew 20, we see Jesus speaking to His disciples after they were bickering over who would be the greatest disciple. Again, we see it is our human nature to be boastful. Jesus then states, "whoever wants to become great among you must be your servant, and whoever wants to be first must be your slave— just as the Son of Man did not come to be served, but to serve, and to give his life as a ransom for many" (Matthew 20:26-28, NIV). He reminded His disciples and us today that in His Kingdom being great means being a servant. This is why the Kingdom of God is sometimes referred to as the Upside-Down Kingdom by theologians. The world we live in today tells us that in order to be great we must have a successful career, have a lot of money, buy the newest and best clothes, electronics, cars, etc. On the flip side, the Upside-Down Kingdom of Christ tells us that we must be humble, seek first the Kingdom, fix our eyes on Jesus, and serve Him. And while the first option may sound more exciting, it is temporary and the happiness that comes with it eventually fades, but Christ's Kingdom will last forever and He will satisfy your every need through His good grace. We need to seek and follow Christ's example in servanthood if we want to become more like Him in our journey of discipleship.

Let's briefly look at a few more examples of Christ demonstrating His servanthood. As we look at Christ's ministry as a whole, we see that He placed a great emphasis on serving His Father and the people He came in contact with. One amazing example of His servant leadership is found in John 13. Some of you may already know the passage I am referring to. Hours before crucifixion, Jesus was with His disciples, partaking in the Passover Festival when He did the unthinkable. Jesus, the King of Kings, knelt down to wash His disciples feet. Back in the days of Christ, foot washing was reserved for lowly servants and was not a delightful task, and definitely not a task a King should be participating in. Yet, we see here that the One who should have been having His feet washed was the One doing the washing. He took on the job a servant would do to prove that He was in fact a servant King who loved His disciples.

Perhaps Jesus' most powerful example of servanthood was His sacrificial death on the cross. His death on the cross proved His love for us and He served us by taking the penalty of sin upon Himself that we may become children of God. I love how Paul talks of Jesus' servanthood in Philippians 2. He says, "Your attitude should be the same as that of Christ Jesus: Who, being in very nature God, did not consider equality with God something to be grasped, but made himself nothing, taking the very nature of a servant, being made in human likeness. And being found in appearance as a man, he humbled himself and became obedient to death – even death on a cross! Therefore God exalted him to the highest place and gave him the name that is above every name, that at the name of Jesus every knee should bow, in heaven and on earth and under the earth, and every tongue confess that Jesus Christ is Lord, to the glory of God the Father" (Philippians 2:6-11, NIV). Servanthood was a characteristic Christ possessed from His early ministry to His final breath on the cross. If we want to grow in Christlikeness, we too must possess the quality of servanthood in our lives and in our ministries.

Cultivating a Servant's Heart

We've already seen how serving doesn't come naturally to us, yet if our desire is to become like Christ, we need to live a humble life and be willing to serve. In order to do this, we must cultivate a servant's heart which may take some time. What exactly does it mean to cultivate the heart of a servant?

To cultivate the heart of a servant, we need to personally know the perfect Servant and follow His lead. We see through Scripture that Jesus' ministry was motivated entirely out of love. Everything He did in His ministry was driven out of the love He had for His Father and for mankind. He came to show us what the Father's love looked like on earth. The greatest example of His love for the world was the sacrifice He made on Calvary being brutally beaten and nailed to the cross with the entire world's sin on His shoulders then miraculously being raised from the dead three days later, ultimately conquering sin and death. He was and still is the perfect sacrifice to reconcile us back to the Father and it was all motivated out of His infinite love. Christ is the perfect example of how serving others stems from first a love for God and then a love for His neighbors (all of mankind). Therefore, our driving motive to serve must first be out of our love for God and second out of love for our neighbors, as this indeed is the greatest commandment in life as Jesus tells us in Mark 12:30-31. When we show love to others in our serving, we are ultimately showing them the love of Christ in a tangible way.

Jesus not only served out of love, but He also served in humility. He didn't care if He would be recognized or rewarded by the world's standards for His service because He knew His greatest reward would be in heaven. Paul reminded his readers in Philippi that Jesus, Who was fully God and fully man, humbled Himself and became obedient to death on the cross (Philippians 2:8).

Everything Jesus did in His earthly ministry was with a humble attitude. He didn't serve the people around Him with arrogance and pride, but with a humble heart filled with grace and truth. Throughout Scripture we see a stark contrast between the ministry of Jesus and the ministry of the Pharisees and other religious leaders in that culture. The Pharisees were well respected religious leaders in the Jewish community who were known for keeping God's laws and commandments. While they did try and keep God's commands, their legalistic mindset hindered them from living the way God wanted them to live.

The Pharisees may have thought they were great role models for the community, but actually they were stumbling blocks all because of their arrogant attitude. They had all the head knowledge, but they were missing it in their heart. Jesus often addressed their behavior through the parables He taught. For example, in Luke 15 Jesus is teaching a series of parables to a crowd which consisted of tax collectors and sinners to which the Pharisees and scribes were not pleased with. In the parable of the lost son, Jesus correlates the characteristics of the older brother to the Pharisees and scribes and the younger brother to the sinners and tax collectors.[10] The whole point of this parable was to show that we all are sinners in need of God's grace, but we must choose how we respond to the invitation of salvation. It all comes down to what is in our hearts. We can know the Father and His Word in our head and still be distant from Him like the older brother or we can admit our sins with a humble heart and draw near to Him like the younger brother. When we have opportunities to serve, may we not become like the Pharisees and serve out of obligation and a distant heart. Instead, let's serve humbly and willingly with a heart focused solely on the glory of God. This is true in our daily lives too. We need to have the same attitude as Jesus when serving and be careful not to make it about getting recognized or receiving rewards for our good deeds.

Another way we cultivate a servant's heart is by being compassionate to those we come in contact with. Jesus' ministry was marked by His great compassion for others. In the Gospel accounts we often see Jesus' compassion was attributed to Him whenever He healed people or did miracles. Scripture tells us that Jesus, who is both fully God and fully man, is the High Priest who is able to sympathize in our weaknesses yet He is without sin (Hebrews 4:15). Throughout His earthly ministry, Jesus showed compassion to those who were considered outcasts and the lowly in His era. For example, back in Jesus' day, those who had ailments or diseases such as leprosy and lameness were often looked down upon by people in their society and isolated. We see in Scripture that Jesus does not follow society's lead, but instead extends compassion and love to those who need it most.

There are so many examples of Jesus showing compassion to those around Him and it is through His example that we must strive to live out in our daily lives. There are many opportunities in our culture today to reach out and show compassion to others. Whether it be to help our neighbors with mundane tasks or extending our hands to help those who are underprivileged in our communities, there are ways to show the compassion of Jesus to those around us. How much better would this world be if we all took the initiative to show compassion and love to everyone around us as Jesus did and still does? The world would be a much better place, but it all begins with us. Seek out opportunities where you can actively show compassion to those around you and use those opportunities to tell of the most compassionate Person you've ever met: Jesus!

When we serve God and others out of love, humility, and compassion, we are showing the world around us what it means to be the hands and feet of Jesus. We are putting Jesus on display through our words and our actions. May we never forget that when we serve others in this way, we are not serving out of our own strength and power, but completely out of God's strength and power. When we serve, we must remember that Jesus is the One we are emulating, not other believers. When we begin comparing our service to others, we miss out on the significance of Whom we are serving. May we always strive to serve in a way that is pleasing to God alone.

Choosing the Good Part

Serving is an important part in the lives of believers as it is something that helps us to grow in Christlikeness. However, one thing we need to be cautious of in our serving is that we don't lose focus on Who it is we are serving. While our intentions in serving are good, sometimes we can overlook the main reason we are serving: to glorify God. In Scripture we see a perfect example of this in the story of Martha and Mary.

Let's look at Luke 10:38-42 for just a moment. In this passage, Luke tells us that Martha welcomed Jesus into her home and there her sister Mary sat at Jesus' feet, listening to His word. Martha, on the other hand, was distracted with much serving and appears to be discouraged with how Mary is not helping her serve then proceeds to complain to Jesus saying, "Lord, do You not care that my sister has left me to serve alone? Therefore tell her to help me" (Luke 10:40). Martha probably thinks Jesus is going to tell Mary to help her serve, but quite the opposite happens and Jesus ends up rebuking her stating, "Martha, Martha, you are worried and troubled about many things. But one thing is needed, and Mary has *chosen the good part*, which will not be taken away from her" (Luke 10:41-42, *emphasis mine*).

Through this passage, we can see that Martha had good intentions in her serving; however, it distracted her and shifted her focus away from Whom she was serving. In contrast, we see that Mary had her heart and mind focused completely on Jesus as she sat at His feet soaking in His words. Though it may not have looked like she was doing as much as Martha, Jesus said that Mary was the one who had chosen the good part. I know I have a tendency to be like Martha sometimes where I get so caught up in serving that I overlook Whom I am ultimately serving. I need to be intentional about being more like Mary and sitting at Jesus' feet, soaking in His precious words. Only when I do this will my serving be most effective.

Ways We Can Serve

Now that we've looked at cultivating a servant's heart, let's look at ways in which we can put that into practice. While this is not going to be an exhaustive list, here are some practical ways in which you can serve God by serving others:

1. Helping your family
   Family is your first and most important ministry opportunity. Whether it's helping your spouse do something as simple as folding the laundry or taking your aging parents to go get groceries, your service doesn't go unnoticed. When you help and serve your family, you are showing them what the hands and feet of Jesus look like. Try to do so on a daily basis and in doing so don't miss the opportunity to share the gospel with family members who may not know Jesus.

2. Volunteering at your church
   When you serve in the local church, you are actively engaging in the Body of Christ. Look for ways in which you can serve in your church that you may show the love of Christ to the

community around you. God has equipped each and every one of us with gifts and talents that are unique to us. Find out what those gifts and talents are and use them to serve your church. If you don't know what spiritual gifts you have, I would recommend asking a mentor or someone close in your life who is a fellow believer and see what they say as they know you more personally. There are also spiritual gift tests online that you can take that can help you indicate what your gifts are so that you can use them to the glory of God.

Also, do not be discouraged if your spiritual gifts change over time. That just means you are growing in grace! I took plenty of spiritual gifts tests during my time in college and while some stayed the same, others changed and that is totally fine. For example, one of my consistent gifts is encouragement, but one that changed was evangelism because my desire for missions grew during my four years at NGU. Overall, whatever gifts you feel God has blessed you with, strive to use them to further the Kingdom of God.

3. Giving to the underprivileged

In Scripture, Jesus placed a lot of emphasis on caring for the needs of those who are poor, sick, or at a disadvantage in life. We read in the Bible that Christ Himself had a deep passion for serving those who were looked down upon in society. We see Him healing the sick and communing with those who were labeled as sinners and tax collectors, just to name a few. Jesus crossed socio-economic barriers to ensure that they could hear the Good News He came to bring. This calling is true for us today. While the world around us may question why we are spending time with those our culture views as insignificant, we know that Christ has called us to love them as He loves them. Take a look at the city you currently live in and think of ways in which you can serve and be a blessing to those who are labeled as "less fortunate." How can you be a blessing to someone in need today and share the love of Jesus while doing so?

Conclusion

In a world that is filled with selfish ambitions and boastfulness, let's stand out and humble ourselves by living a life that is marked with servanthood. Though we may be ridiculed for doing so, may we not lose sight of the One whom we are serving. Service requires sacrifice. Through this chapter we've seen this through the life of Christ. His service cost Him His life. We, as disciples, are called to do the same. We may not die a physical death on the cross, but Christ calls us to take up our cross daily and follow Him (Matthew 16:24). Our daily surrender to His servant leadership allows us to serve Him and others joyfully by the power and the presence of the Holy Spirit. Seek out opportunities to be a blessing and serve others in your community on a daily basis. When our motivation is in line with God's desires, then others will see Christ through us and may even prompt them to want to know Him personally.

CHAPTER 4 REFLECTION QUESTIONS

1. What are some ways we can cultivate a servant's heart?

2. Jesus is our perfect example of what humble servanthood looks like. How can you serve others this week to show and share Jesus' love?

3. As we saw through the story of Martha and Mary, sometimes we have a tendency to be more like Martha and focus on serving rather than Whom we are serving. Do you have the tendency to be more like Martha or Mary when you are serving? If you are more like Martha, how can you shift your focus and be more like Mary?

5
GROWING THROUGH MISSIONS

As we journey through our process of sanctification, we must realize that we as believers all have a common purpose to fulfill while we are living on this earth. It's a purpose that the Lord Himself commands us to do. It's a purpose that we must not take lightly, because the eternity of other people is on the line. That purpose is this: to go and make disciples of all nations (Matthew 28:19). As Christians, we all have the unique purpose and high calling of living a life on mission and spreading the good news of Jesus to all people. Our God is a missionary God and we are called to be His missionary people.

Contrary to what most people perceive missions to be, it is not merely a trip that we take once or twice a year to a faraway land sharing the gospel of Christ; rather, it is a lifestyle that should be integrated in the lives of all believers. We are the instruments God chooses to use to spread His message. He could have chosen a different way for the gospel to be preached, but He didn't. By His grace He chose us who are broken, yet redeemed people, to carry on His gospel to the ends of the earth. This is why we need to take missions so seriously. There are souls in this world who are lost and in some places unreached who are in desperate need to hear the gospel of Christ, but how can they do so if we don't go and tell them?

Paul writes this convicting truth in Romans 10 as he talks about Israel's need for the gospel, "For 'whoever calls on the name of the LORD shall be saved.' How then shall they call on Him in whom they have not believed? And how shall they believe in Him of whom they have not heard? And how shall they hear without a preacher? And how shall they preach unless they are sent? As it is written: 'How beautiful are the feet of those who preach the gospel of peace, who bring glad tidings of good things!' But they have not all obeyed the gospel. For Isaiah says, 'LORD, who has believed our report?' So then faith comes by hearing, and hearing by the word of God" (Romans 10:13-17). Did you catch all the questions Paul raises in this passage? We, as the Church, are all called to be sent out and spread the gospel, whether it's in our hometown or on the other side of the globe. We have an important task to spread the Good News that transforms lives. David Platt writes the following statement about God's missional plan in his book *Radical: Taking Back Your Faith from the American Dream*, "We are the plan of God, and there is no plan B. Of course, God has the power to write the gospel in letters across the clouds that all people can learn about Jesus and believe in him. But in his infinite wisdom, he has not chosen this route. Instead he has chosen to use us as ambassadors who carry the gospel to people who have never heard the name of Jesus…God clearly has decided to use the church - and only the church - as the means by which his gospel will go to the ends of the earth."[11]

We know our mission is to make disciples of all nations, and the goal of this chapter is to explain how we can do that. I am going to structure this chapter around the missional verse found in Acts 1:8, which reads

"But you shall receive power when the Holy Spirit has come upon you; and you shall be witnesses to Me in Jerusalem, and in all Judea and Samaria, and to the end of the earth." This verse is significant because these words were spoken from Jesus Himself before He ascended back into heaven after His crucifixion and resurrection. Essentially, these were His very last words to His disciples, meaning they were extremely important. We see through Acts 1:8 that our God is a missional God and we are called to be missional people. Just as Jesus told His followers that they were to be witnesses of Him to all the world, we too have the same commandment. This chapter will be broken into sections to help us understand how missions is important in our hometown, across our nation, and across the globe.

The Difference Between Lost and Unreached

I mentioned above that there are souls out in the world who are lost and in some places unreached who are in need of the truth of the gospel, but what exactly do the words lost and unreached mean? When we refer to people being lost, we are referring to someone who does not have a relationship with Jesus, but has access to the gospel message. For example, here in America all people have access to the gospel message through the First Amendment, which includes the freedom of religion. Biblically sound churches can be found all across America, especially in the South, where there appears to be a church on nearly every corner, which is why it is commonly known as the 'Bible Belt'. Yet, there are some who still do not have a saving faith in Christ because they choose not to. They have access to churches and the Bible, and yet they still do not believe.

On the other hand, unreached people are those who live in countries where the gospel is not so easily accessible. Those who live in these countries usually practice another religion and do not have biblically sound churches nearby to hear the truth of the gospel. This is why foreign missionaries are needed long term in these places, to bring the truth of the gospel to a people group that has never heard it before. According to the Joshua Project, there are a total of 7.91 billion people on this earth, 3.34 billion of which are considered unreached. That is an astonishing 42.3% of the total population that has never even heard of the gospel.[12] 42.3% of people have never heard the gospel story, never read the Bible, nor have ever attended a church where the gospel had been preached. Many of these people groups live in what is known as the 10/40 Window. The Joshua Project states that "the 10/40 Window is the rectangular area of North Africa, the Middle East and Asia approximately between 10 degrees north and 40 degrees north latitude" and is commonly called "The Resistant Belt" due to the other religions that are practiced like Hinduism, Buddhism, and Islam.[13] Though it may be difficult to reach these people groups, we must obey our call to go and make disciples of all nations.

Those who are lost and those who are unreached are both equally in need of the gospel and it is our job as Christians to share with them the best news they will ever hear. Each soul matters to God and whether people are lost or unreached, He wants His gospel shared with them so that they may find saving faith through Christ Jesus. We, therefore, are

God's chosen instruments to share this good news with both the lost and unreached. Each one of us has a calling to go out and make disciples, whether that be across the street or across the globe. While we act as God's instruments in this very important mission, please be aware that it is not by our own power that people are saved, it is by God's power and will alone. In 1 Corinthians 3, Paul demonstrates how he and his co-laborer, Apollos were merely instruments in God's plan of redemption by stating, "I planted, Apollos watered, but God gave the increase. So then neither he who plants is anything, nor he who waters, but God who gives the increase" (1 Corinthians 3:6-7).

Missions Across the Street

When most people think of the term *missions,* they probably picture a remote village in a jungle somewhere spreading the gospel to people who have never heard of the name of Jesus. And while that is happening somewhere in the world, missions do not just happen in foreign lands. As believers we have the incredible opportunity to do mission work wherever we are, even right here in the town you call home. In fact, it is what we are called to do.

Let's refer back to Acts 1:8 for just a moment. After Jesus promises the power of the Holy Spirit on His disciples, He first tells them that they will be witnesses to Jerusalem. Many correlate this to missions in one's hometown because Jerusalem was the city where the disciples lived. Jesus knew the importance of the gospel being spread not only to foreign places, but also to the place in which He Himself walked and did ministry. Just as the disciples had the task to take the gospel to their hometown, so do we.

I live in what most people refer to as the Bible Belt of the United States, meaning most of the states in the south have church buildings that seem to be on every corner. For example, I can think of at least four churches on the road I live on within a three mile radius. Though there are a couple of different denominations, they all gather each Sunday and worship the risen King. Growing up in such an area where the gospel seems so prominent, I sometimes wonder "how can I effectively share the gospel with a community that seems so involved in church?"

I never really thought of ways I could share the gospel in the community around me until I took a missions class my last semester at Southeastern. One of the weekly assignments that semester really challenged me in how I viewed and did missions in my hometown. The assignment was to find someone each week who you did not think was a Christian and begin a conversation with them with the end goal of sharing the gospel with them if we could. I must say, it was very hard finding people who weren't Christians and I did not find a single person in a span of ten weeks who did not proclaim to be a believer.

While I did not find an unbeliever the whole ten weeks I had the assignment, I did realize that an effective way to start a gospel conversation was to build relationships with people. That is our goal as the body of Christ, to build relationships with people that we may share His Good News with them. You don't have to be in a church building to participate in missions, though that is a possibility. If you are a born again believer, then missions go wherever you go as Jesus gave the Great Commandment to every Christian. The call to go starts right where you are whether it be in your home, your workplace, your school, or the community around you. Wherever God has placed you is your mission field and though it sounds intimidating, just remember you carry the Good News with you and the Holy Spirit will equip you when you need to share it. Trust Him!

I became a Christian in 2011 and for a long time I didn't understand the concept of missions. It wasn't until I was in college when God began revealing to me what being on mission actually meant and how I didn't have to go overseas to do so. I began developing a heart for missions the summer of 2016 (which would have been before starting my sophomore year of college). That summer, God opened up an opportunity for me to serve in a very small local church that was hosting Vacation Bible School (VBS) to the children in their community.

This church did not have many members so a student mission team from the coast of South Carolina came to volunteer and help facilitate the lessons for the week and prayer walk in the community. I realized that though I did not travel hours away from home to help, it was still a mission trip for me regardless and an experience that changed my life forever. As I helped each night at this VBS, I began to realize the need for the gospel in my own community. Some of the children who attended were probably hungry and some didn't even have extra pairs of shoes. It was heartbreaking seeing the physical needs of some of these children that lived in my hometown. What was even more heartbreaking was knowing that they each had a deeper need, a spiritual need, which was to know the love and gospel of Jesus. And that is why missions are needed, friends. There are deep spiritual needs in the lives of people around you in your own community that only Jesus can meet, but we must act as His messengers so that they may come to saving faith in Him.

Though mission work seems more prominent in a foreign context, never forget the significance of gospel work in your own community. Your routine life may seem mundane and insignificant, but Christ can use you wherever you are whether it be in your own home, in your school, in your workplace, in your neighborhood, or in your community. Through the empowerment of the Holy Spirit, missions go wherever you go. My challenge to you today is to seek out opportunities around you where you can build relationships with intentions to share the gospel with others in your life.

Missions Across the Nation

It's true that mission work is needed in our hometowns, but have you thought about missions in other parts of the nation? When we look at Acts 1:8, Jesus mentions to His disciples that they are to be witnesses not only to Jerusalem, their hometown, but also to Judea and Samaria, which were neighboring regions to Jerusalem. Similar to Acts 1:8, we are to bring the gospel to our neighboring regions as well.

If you live in the United States, you may notice there are some states that do not have a prominent Christian presence. This is the reason why national missions are important. We would consider these parts of

America as the lost population whether it be due to their cultural or spiritual differences or both. International missions doesn't have to happen overseas, it can happen in America in big, populated cities. I didn't realize this until I went on my first national mission trip.

In 2017, my love for mission work began to grow and I felt God calling me to take a leap of faith and travel to another state to share the love of Jesus. This was huge for me because at that point in my life I had never been to another state without my parents. As I began praying and seeking God, my university had mission trips coming up that Spring and one of them was to New York City. My first initial thought was how exciting going to New York City would be and I pictured myself walking around Times Square staring up at the skyscrapers. After a few team meetings, I knew that is not what this trip was going to be like at all. I discovered that we would be ministering to people from all over the world in Queens by teaching them English and providing Bible studies.

As we went through our training and discussed the statistics of the people we would be working with, I was amazed at how many people groups were represented in the city of Queens and how diverse it was. When we first set foot in Queens, it was almost a culture shock, because each street was represented by a different country. For example one street would be known as "Little India," while a couple streets over would be "Little China." I was amazed at how many people groups were represented in this city and I didn't even have to leave the country.

One of the many things I learned from this trip was that some of the students who became Christians through the ESL ministry would often go back to their home country and spread the gospel to their family and friends. Keep in mind that the countries they came from are not receptive to the gospel like America is, so the fact that they would go back home and share the Good News of Jesus is amazing! The ministry we do here in America may affect a community or a culture, but friends let's not forget it can even affect the world.

National missions is such a blessing to so many and there is an organization I want you to be aware of as you pray about your next step in national missions. If you're of the Southern Baptist denomination you probably already know which organization I am about to refer to. It's called the North American Mission Board (NAMB) and its goal is to support North American missionaries through prayer and financial support. Each Easter season, the North American Mission Board takes up an offering known as the Annie Armstrong Easter Offering. This annual offering supports national missionaries all over the United States and Canada. Not only can you give financially to support national missionaries, but you can also pray for them. Through prayer, we are interceding on their behalf and supporting them on a deeper, more spiritual level that only God can do.

Missions Across the World

We as believers are not only called to spread the gospel in our hometown and nation, but also around the world. When we refer back to our passage in Acts 1:8, we see that Christ gave His disciples the important task to be witnesses "to the ends of the earth." That sounds like a daunting task, doesn't it? However, we know that through the work of the Holy Spirit, this task can and will be accomplished. One day before the throne of God, people from every tribe, tongue, and nation will be praising God proclaiming, "Salvation belongs to our God who sits on the throne, and to the Lamb!" (Revelation 7:9-10). We also know that once the gospel is preached in the whole world, the end will come and Christ will return (see Matthew 24:14). Through the work of the Holy Spirit in our lives, God has chosen us to be His vessel in spreading the Good News of Jesus to people all over the world. This is a task that should not be taken lightly. Whether we feel called to go overseas and become full-time missionaries or go on short-term mission trips or support missionaries through financial means, we are called to take the gospel to all nations.

Though I am not a full-time missionary or feel God is calling me to do so, I do have a heart for international missions. I've been on two international mission trips and both deeply impacted my love and passion for missions. My first trip was to Bangkok, Thailand in May of 2018 and it was an eye-opening experience I will never forget. I honestly didn't know what to expect as my team and I traveled to the other side of the globe. I remember as we landed feeling so nervous, yet so excited that we would soon be sharing the gospel of Jesus with those who have never even heard of His name. Thailand falls within the "10/40 Window" I mentioned earlier in this chapter as a majority of the population are considered unreached, meaning they've never heard of Jesus. In Thailand, the predominant religion is Buddhism.

The Buddhist religion runs so deep in Thai culture that even their identity is wrapped up in it. We learned quickly that "to be Thai is to be

Buddhist" and if they turn away from Buddhism and convert to another faith such as Christianity, then most likely their families would disown them. This is exactly what happened with one of our translators. Once she converted to Christianity, her parents disowned her. While she said that was difficult, you could tell she was happy with her decision in following Christ. Seeing someone so confident in her relationship with Jesus really reminded me that when we have Christ at the center of our lives, we have all we need and no one can take that joy away from us. Life may be difficult at times as God never promised us an easy life, but we can rest assured that with Christ in our lives, we can face those uncertainties with great joy and peace. Our translator's life and testimony was on full display to her fellow Thai friends through how she lived with such joy.

Another thing I learned through my trip to Thailand was that people are much more receptive to hearing the gospel of Christ. I feel like it is sometimes more difficult here in America to share the gospel, because it is so common and some people may already have preconceived notions about it. In Thailand, however, the gospel was brand new for most of them. One of our main tasks in Bangkok was teaching English as a second language. Those who signed up for the class were first taught the basics of the English language like the alphabet, letters, numbers, colors, etc. However, each lesson ended with a Bible lesson, beginning in Genesis so by the end of the week they heard the full gospel message in a simplistic way. It was amazing to see some of them grapple with how God loves them so much that He sent Jesus to die on the cross for our sins. They were amazed that there is a God who would do such a thing. Though I am unsure if any accepted Jesus during our time there, I know there were a few who wanted to know more and I sure do pray that they will indeed come to know the Lord Jesus on a personal level.

Through international missions, I have learned that the proclaiming of the gospel is so desperately needed to a spiritually dying world. There are thousands of people groups who have never even heard His name and it is our duty to take the Good News to them. Our call to go is an important calling that shouldn't be dismissed. Although every believer is not called to go overseas, there are some practical ways in which we can participate in international missions. Here are a few ways:

1. Go on a short-term or long-term trip:
   One of the most eye-opening experiences about missions I've ever had has been on trips overseas. Experiencing a different culture really helps you understand the deep need for the gospel. While traveling abroad is not for everyone, I want to encourage you to pray about opportunities in which you can be a part of to experience the uniqueness of going and sharing the Good News with lost and unreached people groups.

2. The Lottie Moon Christmas Offering:
   Similar to NAMB, the International Mission Board also has an annual offering each December that is designated specifically for international missions. The offering is named after Lottie Moon, a female missionary who spent her missionary career

serving in China. Each Christmas season, the offering is emphasized in Southern Baptist Churches and collected throughout the month of December. 100% of proceeds collected go toward supporting missionaries overseas.

3. Praying for missionaries:
Financial support of missionaries is great, but spiritually supporting missionaries is even better. Praying for missionaries overseas is a great way to participate in international missions. Through interceding on behalf of foreign missionaries, we know God can and will do amazing things in the lives of others who have yet to hear His name.

4. Praying for the unreached:
Another way we can participate in the Great Commision is by praying for those who are unreached. One resource I would like you to be aware of is the Joshua Project.[14] The Joshua Project is a website that lists people groups and nations that need to hear the gospel, offering information about them and even has specific prayer points to help guide you. Satan's grip is tight and spiritual darkness is looming on nations where the gospel is not being proclaimed. As believers, we know prayer is powerful, so let's spend time praying for those in other nations that their eyes may be opened "in order to turn them from darkness to light, and from the power of Satan to God" (Acts 26:18a).

Living a Life on Mission

We've seen throughout this chapter that missions are an important task in the life of every believer. We've seen through Acts 1:8 that Jesus has called each of us to be His witness whether that be in our hometown, in our nation, or overseas. While a majority of us are not vocational missionaries, we are tasked to participate in sharing the Good News wherever we go. In this section, we will look at what it means to live a life on mission for Christ.

You may not be a vocational missionary, but have you considered that your mission field is wherever God has placed you? We as believers have an important role to play even in our daily, sometimes mundane lives. Peter reminds his audience of this truth in his first letter, "But you are a chosen generation, a royal priesthood, a holy nation, His own special people, that you may proclaim the praises of Him who called you out of darkness into His marvelous light" (1 Peter 2:9). The same is true of us today. We are a chosen generation, called to proclaim His praises and we are to do this wherever we are.

Whatever your vocation is, the gospel is needed there even if you may not be openly able to share it. If you are a believer, the life you live is a reflection of Christ Himself to the world around you. That means your family, friends, coworkers, students, or whoever is around you will see Christ on display by how you love through your words and actions. Jesus said in John 13:35, "By this all will know that you are My disciples, if you have love for one another." Therefore, love is our ultimate motive in our mission driven life. Through loving God and loving others, all will know that we are His disciples. Your mission field is all around you. The gospel is needed everywhere you go. I want to challenge you this week to, seek ways in which you can share the gospel with those around you and always live in such a way that Christ's love can be seen through you.

Conclusion

There's no doubt that we as believers are called by God to participate in the Great Commission: to go and make disciples of all nations. We've seen throughout this chapter that missions is more than merely a short-term trip, rather it is a lifestyle that needs to be cultivated in the lives of Christians. With the Holy Spirit in our hearts, we are equipped to share the gospel wherever we are, whether that be in our homes, in our workplaces, or even in a foreign land. Your mission field is wherever you go!

CHAPTER 5 REFLECTION QUESTIONS

1. Before reading this chapter, what did you picture missions being?

2. How has your view on missions changed (if any) after reading this chapter?

3. What are some practical ways you can live your life on mission for God? Who can you share the gospel with this week?

Part Three
Glorification

We Will Be Saved

In our journey of discipleship, we have seen how it all begins the day we trust in Jesus as our Savior and continues through sanctification, the process of becoming holy. We will never become holy as God is holy in this life, but what if I told you that our longing to be like Christ will come to fruition soon enough? That's right, the day God will restore everything back to His original design will be the day we will be like our Savior and live with Him for eternity.

This last section of this book will focus on glorification. Glorification is the last part of our journey as believers and will happen at the Second Coming of Christ. Glorification means that those who have placed their faith in Christ will be saved from their sins forever. As we've used the plant/flower analogy in the last two sections, I'm going to use it once again. Throughout our discipleship journey, we have seen how our faith is a seed rooted in salvation, and that seed needs nourishment to grow, so through sanctification we watch the seed grow upward taking shape and striving to become the beautiful tree it's meant to be.

Now, as we look at the final stage of our journey through glorification, let's imagine our tree again for just a moment. This tree has been through a lot during its lifetime, but one day it will finally reach its full potential and bear the fruit it had been longing to bear. In the coming kingdom, we will be made new. Our long journey of becoming like Christ here on earth will finally come to fruition, because we will finally be like Him. Our root, that started the moment of our conversion will finally bloom and, while our journey in sanctification comes to an end, our journey as glorified lifelong worshipers of the King begins!

6
COMING TO FRUITION IN THE COMING KINGDOM

In our journey so far, we've seen that each day from the moment we are saved, we strive to become more like Jesus by growing in His grace and knowledge. Our journey in discipleship will eventually come to an end and it will happen the day Christ returns to restore completely all which was broken and tainted by sin. That's right, one day we will not be striving to become more like Jesus because through His grace, we will finally be like Him.

The Coming Kingdom

Imagine a place where everything is perfect. In this place there is no more pain, no more tears, no more death, no more suffering. Sounds unbelievable right? But guess what? One day it will be a reality. One day, we who are in Christ will experience this perfect place for all eternity. Oh and what a day that will be!

The book of Revelation, written by the apostle John, gives us a glimpse of what the coming Kingdom will be like. As John neared the end of his life on the island of Patmos, God revealed to him what was to be expected in the end times. As believers, we can rest assured that Christ's second coming will be glorious and that we too will be raised up with Him when the trumpet sounds. This is what we are longing for, complete restoration with our King. It's also something we are preparing for. I love how Billy Graham puts it in his book *Peace with God*, "Do you have the hope of the coming again of the Lord Jesus Christ? Then you should live it - a pure life, a godly life, a surrendered life, a consecrated life. There's a sense in which we're sanctified when we receive Christ. There's a sense in which we grow in grace and knowledge of Christ in progressive sanctification. But one day we shall see Jesus face to face, and total sanctification is when we're perfect, as He is perfect. We shall see Him as He is."[15] Essentially, the life we are living today is in preparation for the second coming of Christ, it is the goal in our discipleship journey. The day Christ returns and we are whisked away with Him in heaven, we will be completely made new and the struggles this earthly life brought will be no more.

John also writes in Revelation 21:1-2, "Now I saw a new heaven and a new earth, for the first heaven and the first earth had passed away. Also there was no more sea. Then I, John, saw the holy city, New Jerusalem, coming down out of heaven from God, prepared as a bride adorned for her husband." How incredible it is to know that one day, all God's children will be with Him in a new heaven and new earth where everything is right again. The earth that was once perfect in Genesis but was shortly tainted by sin and death will ultimately be passed away and this new earth will be perfect as God Himself is perfect as well as every believer that has ever lived. Paul explains in 1 Corinthians 15 that at the last trumpet, the believers who are dead will be raised and shall be changed (1 Corinthians 15:52). How amazing it is to know that we will not sleep in our graves forever, but will one day live forever in complete and perfect unity with our Savior. I am so longing for that day.

In writing this chapter, I am finding that I have a new found hope and comfort that all the realities of heaven bring to my soul. As I write this chapter, I recently lost someone in my immediate family, and the sting of death took an emotional toll on me. I had never lost someone close to me before, so learning the depth of the grieving process was a struggle. Though I have faith in Christ and knew my loved one was rejoicing in heaven, grief for my family and myself was still present. While it is normal for us to grieve loss, I am thankful for the hope that the resurrection of Christ promises me – the promise that I will one day not only stand face to face with my precious Savior, but I will also be reunited with loved ones who have gone before me and we will be together forever. This is the hope only the gospel of Jesus can offer.

The Glory of Glorification

There are so many things I am longing for when Christ returns – being reunited with family, obtaining a new body, and not having to experience pain and death, just to name a few. While these things are certainly something to look forward to, we need to be careful in not making the Second Coming about us. The whole purpose of Christ returning to make all things new is not for our gain; rather, it is ultimately for the glory of God. Thankfully, by His goodness, mercy, love, and grace, He grants us incredible benefits for us to enjoy for eternity. God's glory and presence will be the centerpiece of everything that will happen in the new heaven and new earth.

The Apostle John writes in this beautiful description of God's glory on display in the new heaven and earth at the end of Revelation 21, "But I saw no temple in it, for the Lord God Almighty and the Lamb are its temple. The city had no need of the sun or of the moon to shine in it, for the glory of God illuminated it. The Lamb is its light. And the nations of those who are saved shall walk in its light, and the kings of the earth bring their glory and honor into it. Its gates shall not be shut at all by day (there shall be no night there). And they shall bring the glory and the honor of the nations into it. But there shall by no means enter it anything that defiles, or causes an abomination or a lie, but only those who are written in the Lamb's Book of Life" (Revelation 21:22-26).

Through this verse we see God's glory on full display in the new Jerusalem. There will be no more need for a temple or the sun, because God Himself will be the temple in which we dwell and His light will be what illuminates the city. John really places an emphasis on how God's glory will be the ultimate focus in the new heaven and earth. In this broken world we live in today, there's no doubt God's glory is on display all around us; however, due to sin, our vision of His glory is tainted. It can be difficult to see God's glory in a world filled with destruction, death, sorrow, and trials. But praise God that one day we will see His glory with our own eyes without any distractions, fears, or doubts and we will be able to worship Him forever as He originally intended in the Garden of Eden. All brokenness will be restored, sin will be no more, and God will be given the glory He deserves all because of the great love He has shown through us in Christ Jesus who overcame sin and death on our behalf. Hallelujah, what a Savior!

Living in Preparation of the Coming Kingdom

I don't know about you, but I'm not one who is big on surprises. I like having things planned out and strive to execute that plan as best I can. Sometimes I can be a little spontaneous, but more often than not I play it safe and plan ahead. When we think about the Second Coming of Christ, there is a sense of preparation that we must actively pursue while here on earth. The Apostle Paul says that in the twinkling of an eye the last trumpet will sound (1 Corinthians 15:52) meaning it will happen very quickly. On top of that, Jesus even states in Matthew's Gospel account, "But of that day and hour no one knows, not even the angels of heaven, but My Father only" (Matthew 24:36). So not only will the Second Coming be quick, but it will also happen when we least expect it, because no one, not even Jesus, knows when He will return for His children. Therefore, we must live today and each day with the Second Coming in our sights. How do we live in anticipation of the Second Coming?

1. Know in your soul that you are a child of God. Each of us are faced with a very important and eternal choice that we must make while we are alive on this earth. Choice #1: Accept Christ and be reconciled to Him through the gift of the Holy Spirit and enjoy Him forever in heaven. Choice #2: Reject Christ and be separated from Him for all eternity in an awful place called

hell. I pray and I hope you choose to accept Christ and spend eternity with Him. The moment we are saved by grace through faith (as we talked about in chapter 1), we are guaranteed heaven and our souls are perfectly at peace with God.

2. Live each day by growing in grace and knowledge of Christ. Throughout this book, we've seen ways in which we can grow through the process of sanctification as we seek to become more Christlike. Each chapter has pointed us to what pursuing holiness looks like and this helps us also to prepare for the Second Coming. Whether it be through Bible intake, community, serving, or missions, we are living each day with the goal of knowing Christ and making Him known to the world around us. When we live each day with a Kingdom mindset, we are preparing for the Second Coming of Christ. May we strive to live each day the way God had originally intended, to glorify Him and Him alone.

No one knows the day nor hour in which the Son will return, so we must be ready at any moment. Our hearts, minds, and souls need to be focused on God and His glory. While we anticipate the coming of Christ, we must also live with a sense of urgency. We need to be eager and willing to share the gospel with those around us because we do not know when the end will come. God's desire is for all people to come to know Him through a personal relationship and He has chosen us as His instruments as we have seen in chapter five.

Conclusion

As our journey comes to an end, we see the hope that only comes through Christ Himself when He returns. Through the Second Coming, we will be completely restored through the process of glorification where we will see Christ face to face and live with Him forever in a place where no death, pain, or suffering will be present. The ultimate purpose of our glorification is for the glory of God. As we began our journey with justification and strive each day to grow in Christlikeness through sanctification, the more we long for the day where we will be glorified in heaven, finally experiencing what our soul has been longing for since the fall of mankind: to be home and at perfect peace with our God. The life we live today for Christ points us to the glorious perfection we will one day experience.

CHAPTER 6 REFLECTION QUESTIONS

1. How does knowing that one day God will restore everything back to perfection change the way you live for today?

2. Has this book helped you in your pursuit of growing in grace and knowledge of our Lord and Savior Jesus Christ? If so, how?

A Note From the Author

From the moment of our conversion we begin our lifelong discipleship journey. Through sanctification, we strive to grow in grace and knowledge of our Lord Jesus that we may become more like Him in the process, until the day we reach eternity and are made complete through glorification. What a day that will be!

My prayer for us is that as we live each day in the anticipation of the Second Coming, that we will "run with endurance the race that is set before us" (Hebrews 12:1), and "not grow weary while doing good" (Galatians 6:9), that we may represent Christ well to everyone we come in contact with so that they too may come to know Him as the beautiful Savior He is.

I hope this book has encouraged and challenged you as you seek a deeper relationship with King Jesus. I thank God for allowing me to share my heart with you all and I pray this book brings Him glory. Amen!

Acknowledgements

I would like to take some time to say a special thank you to those who have encouraged me and helped me make this book possible.

First and foremost, I would like to thank God. This book wouldn't have even come to be without His grace and guidance. Thank You, God, for being with me at each step of this process and laying on my heart the desire to write such a book. I pray that it brings You all the glory You deserve.

To my mom, Michelle Merck, thank you for your constant encouragement to me throughout this entire process. I admire you so much and I am thankful for your love and support. Thank you for showing me the love of Jesus on a daily basis.

To Ruth McWhite, thank you for taking time out of your busy schedule to review the contents of this book. Thank you for being such a wonderful friend and mentor to me during my college years. I am grateful for you and your ministry.

To Tom Capps, thank you as well for taking time out of your busy schedule to review the contents of this book. I appreciate your friendship and godly leadership. I am thankful for you and your ministry.

To my parents (Michelle and John), my grandparents (Diane and Marion), my family, and my friends who have cheered me on and encouraged me throughout this process, I would like to say thank you to all of you. You mean so much to me and I am thankful to have you in my life.

About the Author

Ashley Merck is a graduate of Southeastern Baptist Theological Seminary ('21) where she holds a Master of Arts in Christian Studies. She also holds a Bachelor of Arts in Digital Media from North Greenville University ('19). She is passionate about women's ministry, but also enjoys writing. During seminary, Ashley felt God leading her to write a book on discipleship and that is how *Growing in Grace: The Journey of Discipleship* came to be. Her prayer is that this book will help and encourage you in your pursuit of godly discipleship.

REFERENCES

INTRODUCTION

[1] Karen Dockery, Johnnie Godwin, and Phyllis Godwin, "Disciple," *The Student Bible Dictionary* (Uhrichsville: Barbour Publishing, 2000), 77.

[2] Some portions from this chart are used from the following article. Jeremy Meyers, "Words that DO NOT Refer to Eternal Life (Part 3): Justification, Sanctification, and Glorification," https://www.redeeminggod.com/eternal-life-3-justification-sanctification-glorification/ (Accessed August 12, 2023).

CHAPTER 1

[3] Matt Chandler, *The Explicit Gospel* (Wheaton, IL: Crossway, 2012), 83.

CHAPTER 2

[4] Robby and Kandi Gallaty, *Foundations: A 260-Day Bible Reading Plan for Busy Teens* (Nashville, TN: Lifeway Resources, 2017), 9-10.

[5] Donald S. Whitney, *Spiritual Disciplines for the Christian Life* (Colorado Springs, CO: NavPress, 2014), 4.

CHAPTER 3

[6] Michael F. Bird, *Evangelical Theology* (Grand Rapids, MI: Zondervan, 2013), 152.

[7] J. Strokuva, "Community," *Evangelical Dictionary of Theology*, 3rd ed. Editors: Daniel J Treier and Walter A Elwell (Grand Rapids, MI: Baker Publishing Group, 2017), 199.

[8] Merriam-Webster Dictionary, "Worship," https://www.merriam-webster.com/dictionary/worship. Accessed December 27, 2022.

[9] Chuck Lawless, *Mentor: How Along-the-Way Discipleship Will Change Your Life* (Nashville, TN: Lifeway Press, 2017), 10.

CHAPTER 4

[10] Timothy Keller, The Prodigal God: Recovering the Heart of the Christian Faith (United States of America: Penguin Books, 2008), 10.

CHAPTER 5

[11] David Platt, *Radical: Taking Back Your Faith from the American Dream* (Orange, CA: Yates & Yates LLP, Attorneys and Counselors, 2010), 156-157.

[12] Information found on https://www.joshuaproject.net (Accessed June 20, 2022).

[13] https://www.joshuaproject.net/resources/articles/10_40_window. (Accessed June 20, 2022).

[14] For more information, resources, and prayer guides, visit https://www.joshuaproject.net/.

CHAPTER 6

[15] Billy Graham, *Peace with God* (Billy Graham Library Selection, 1984), 264.

NOTES

NOTES

NOTES

NOTES

NOTES

Made in the USA
Columbia, SC
15 June 2025